WAITANGI DAY

Philippa Werry

First published in 2015 by New Holland Publishers (NZ) Ltd
Auckland • Sydney • London

www.newhollandpublishers.co.nz

5/39 Woodside Avenue, Northcote, Auckland 0627, New Zealand
Unit 1, 66 Gibbes Street, Chatswood, NSW 2067, Australia
The Chandlery, Unit 9, 50 Westminster Bridge Road, London, SE1 7QY, United Kingdom

Copyright © 2015 in text: Philippa Werry
Copyright © 2015 in photographs and illustrations as credited on page 62
Copyright © 2015 New Holland Publishers (NZ) Ltd
Philippa Werry has asserted her right to be identified as the author of this work.

The author and publisher gratefully acknowledge the assistance of Creative New Zealand

Publishing manager: Christine Thomson
Editor: Matt Turner, Wooden Shed
Design: Nick Turzynski, redinc., book design, Auckland
Map illustrations: Thomas Casey

National Library of New Zealand Cataloguing-in-Publication Data

Werry, Philippa, 1958-
Waitangi Day : the New Zealand story : what it is and why it matters / Philippa Werry.
Includes bibliographical references and index.
ISBN 978-1-86966-421-3
1. Treaty of Waitangi (1840)—Juvenile literature. 2. Waitangi Day—Juvenile literature. 3. New Zealand—History—Juvenile Literature. [1. Tiriti o Waitangi. reo 2. Kōrero nehe. reo].
993—dc 23

3 5 7 9 10 8 6 4 2

Printed in China at Everbest Printing Co, on paper sourced from sustainable forests.

All rights reserved. No part of this publication may be reproduced, stored in a retrieval system, or transmitted in any form or by any means, electronic, mechanical, photocopying, recording or otherwise, without the prior permission of the publishers and copyright holders.

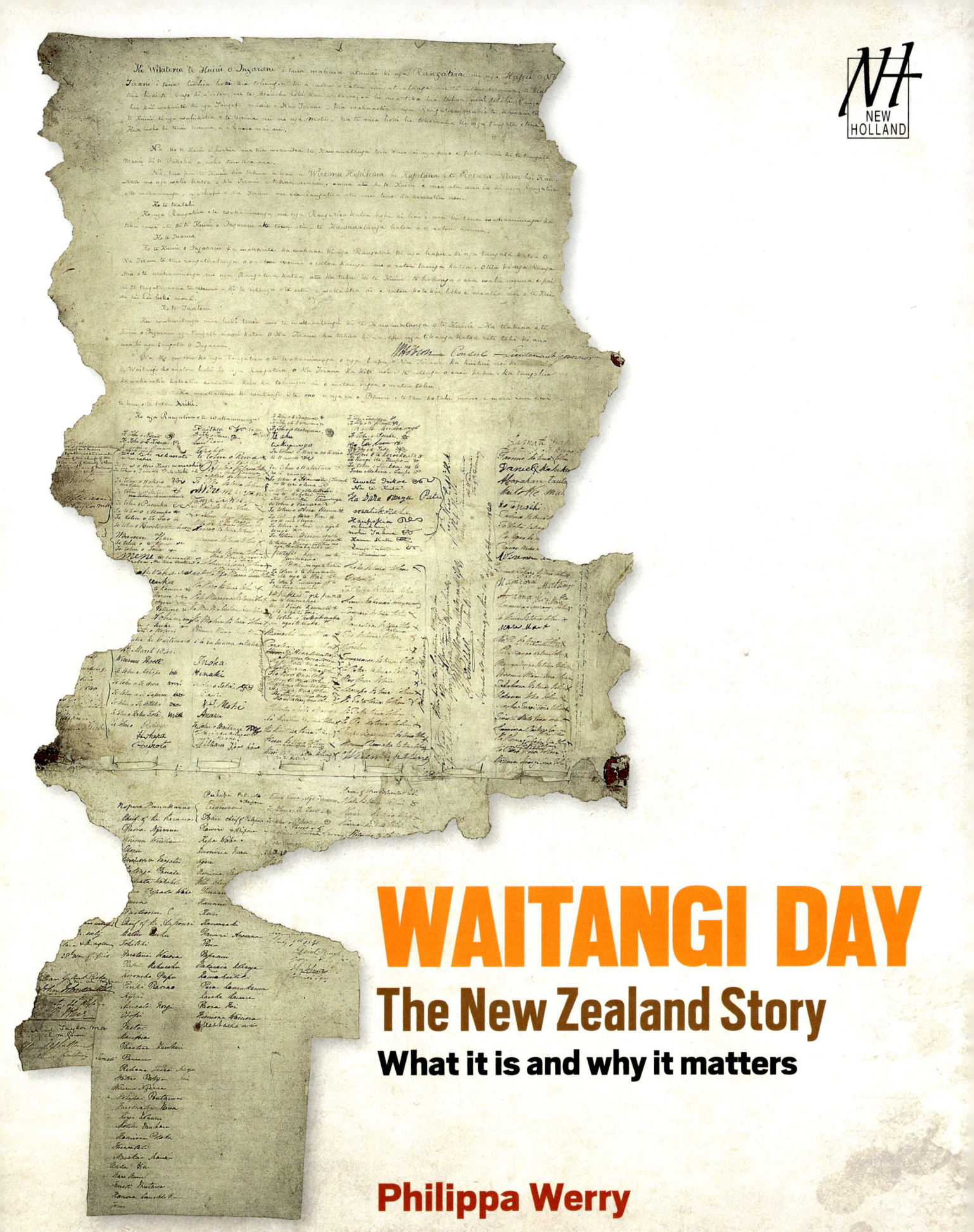

WAITANGI DAY
The New Zealand Story
What it is and why it matters

Philippa Werry

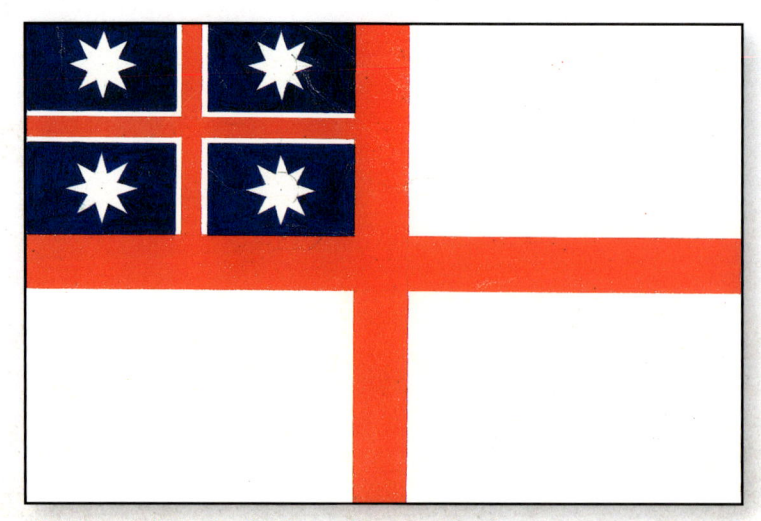

The Flag of the United Tribes of New Zealand.

CONTENTS

Introduction **6**

CHAPTER 1 **EARLY MEETINGS 7**

CHAPTER 2 **WHAT HAPPENED NEXT? 19**

CHAPTER 3 **CHANGE, PROTEST AND PROGRESS 31**

CHAPTER 4 **WAITANGI DAY IN THE 21ST CENTURY 44**

CHAPTER 5 **VISITING WAITANGI: WHAT TO SEE 50**

Glossary **60**

Timeline **60**

Further reading **61**

Picture credits **62**

Index **63**

Acknowledgements **64**

An aerial view of Waitangi, showing Te Whare Rūnanga the Meeting House (with red roof) and the Treaty House, half hidden amongst the trees. The flagpole is on the lawn behind the tall pine tree.

Introduction

What is Waitangi Day?

On 6 February 1840, the Treaty of Waitangi (or Te Tiriti o Waitangi) was first signed at Waitangi in the Bay of Islands.

Today, Waitangi Day is celebrated every year on 6 February. It is a public holiday and the day is marked by events held all over the country (and by New Zealanders overseas).

The Treaty or Te Tiriti is now seen as New Zealand's founding document, but that wasn't always the case. For a long time, the date of 6 February went unnoticed by many people. In more recent years, Waitangi Day has often been linked with protests and debates about its meaning, but we continue to focus on it as a day that is central to the story of our country, our people, and our national identity.

This book tells the history behind Waitangi Day. It explains what the day commemorates, how it has been marked over the years, and why it is important today.

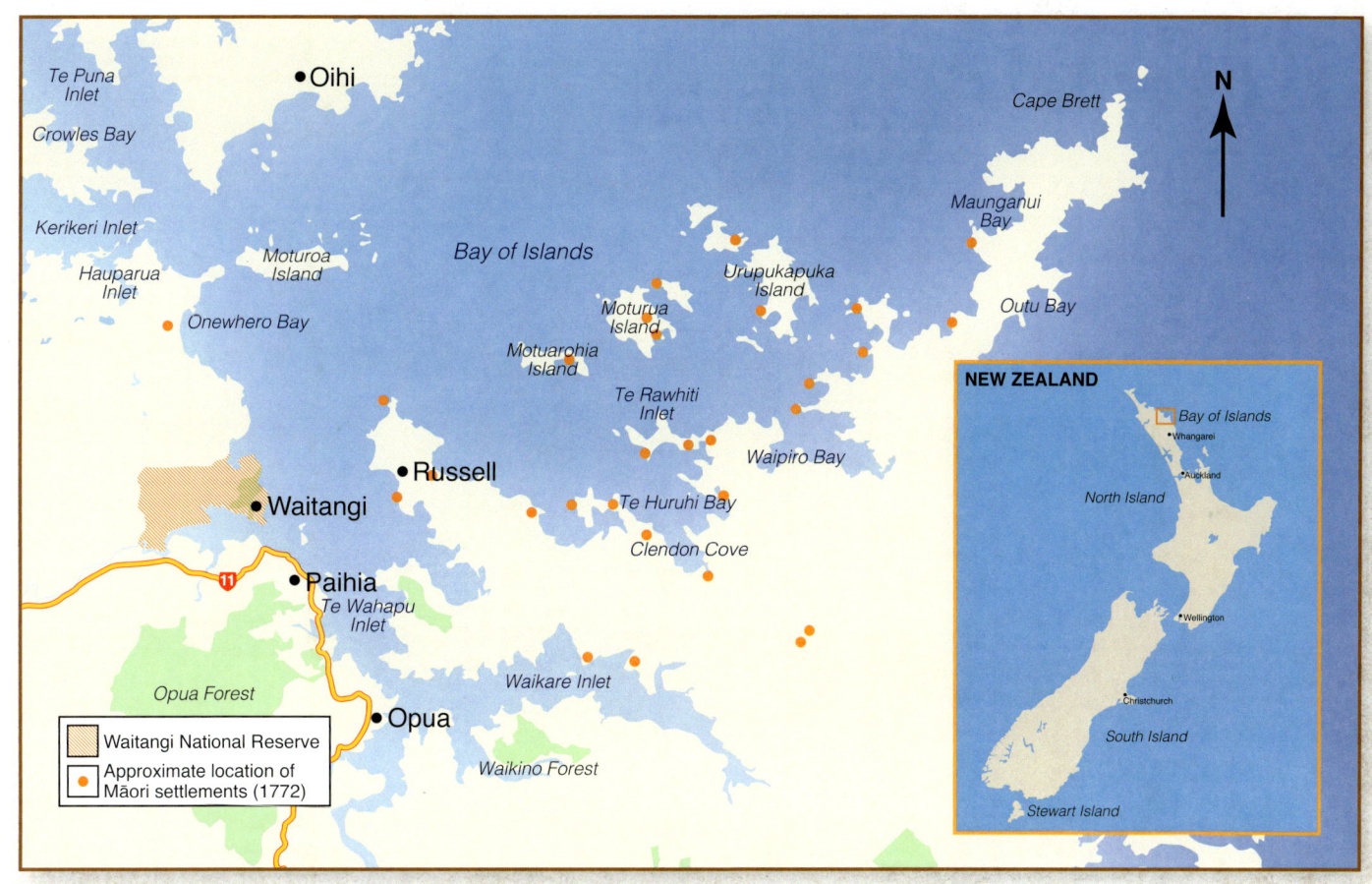

The Bay of Islands, showing early Māori settlements and the Waitangi National Reserve.

CHAPTER 1

EARLY MEETINGS

The Bay of Islands (Te Pēwhairangi)

More than a hundred islands, along with rocky islets, sandy beaches, sheltered bays and harbours, mangroves, rivers and waterfalls, make up the Bay of Islands. This region, one of the first places where Māori and European met, formed the backdrop to the early history of New Zealand.

According to Māori traditional histories, the Bay of Islands was visited over a thousand years ago by Kupe and Ngake (or Ngāhue), the first Polynesian explorers to discover Aotearoa. It became home to the Ngare Raumati and Ngāti Manu iwi. The Ngāpuhi iwi moved into the area from the seventeenth century on. Their tribal area gradually expanded until Ngāpuhi became the largest iwi in New Zealand and they played a crucial part in early Māori–

European relationships.

Archaeologists believe Māori occupied different villages or pā sites in and around Waitangi. The first mention of Waitangi in Māori tradition relates to Maikuku, the daughter of Uenuku and Kareariki a Ngaitohuhu, who lived at Pourua pā. Maikuku, who was very beautiful, went to live in a cave in Waitangi, known as Te Ana o Maikuku. She married a man named Hua and they moved into Ruarangi, a house above the cave, where their first child was born. Maikuku is an ancestor of the people of Ngāpuhi.

European explorers, navigators, scientists and artists

The eighteenth and early nineteenth centuries were a time of ocean-going exploration by leading European nations. England, France and Spain sent ships around the world in a race to discover and claim new territories. Ships' officers and crew mapped and recorded their voyages on charts and in logbooks. Often there were scientists, botanists and artists on board to examine new specimens and to paint or draw the scenery and its inhabitants.

In late November 1769, Captain James Cook of the *Endeavour* anchored off Motuarohia (or Roberton) Island for about a week. Hundreds of local Māori paddled out in canoes to meet the ship. The crew traded with them for fish and collected fresh water, wood, grass for the sheep on board and 'sellery' (native celery) to use against scurvy. Joseph Banks, a rich young scientist who had helped to fund the expedition, climbed a hill and saw 'a most surprizing place: it was full of an innumerable quantity of Islands'. Captain Cook described 'a large and pretty deep Bay'. Later he recorded, 'I have named it the Bay of Islands.'

Marc Joseph Marion du Fresne led a French expedition that arrived in two ships in May 1772. They stayed on Moturua Island and seemed to get on well with local Māori, but a series of apparent misunderstandings resulted in tragedy when 24 officers and men, and du Fresne himself, were attacked and killed. His second in command, Julien Crozet, launched an attack in retaliation that destroyed a pā and killed over 200 Māori. One story tells how before the French ships sailed away, Crozet buried a bottle containing a

This hand-coloured slide shows waka taua (war canoes) and a British yacht, drawn by Henry Williams in 1833–35.

formal document claiming French possession of the land. The directions were precise — '57 paces from the mark of high spring tide and 10 paces from the left bank of the little stream' — but the bottle has never been found.

After du Fresne's death, European visitors kept away from the Bay of Islands for many years. The attacks by local Māori on the *Parramatta* in 1808 and the *Boyd* in 1809 also caused much disquiet and led to more revenge killings — on both sides. But despite hostile encounters such as these (often as a result of broken trust), plenty of other meetings between Māori and Europeans were friendly. Some of the early European arrivals married Māori women and raised families; they became known as 'Pākehā Māori'.

Whalers, sealers and traders

After the first European explorers came the sealers and the whalers. Seal skins were made into fur coats and hats, and the leather into shoes, or the skins could be traded in China for tea. The sealing trade around the South Island was soon over because the gangs slaughtered the seals so ruthlessly, but the whaling ships stayed for much longer.

In addition to the whaling ships, other ships came to

Dutch/English businessman Joel Polack produced this engraving of sperm whales off New Zealand for a book he wrote about his 'travels and adventures' in this country.

trade for natural resources such as flax, timber and kauri gum. Traders and shopkeepers arrived, and so did runaway convicts, sailors, carpenters, boat builders and other craftsmen, in search of a new or different way of life. Some Māori men took jobs on the whaling boats, and others also travelled overseas, including Hongi Hika and Waikato who met King George IV in England.

Kororāreka (now Russell) became a bustling port as boats arrived in need of repairs or supplies. Their crews knew that they could get fresh water and pork, fish, fresh vegetables and wood from local Māori in return for iron, clothing and muskets. Life on board was hard, so when the whalers came ashore, they wanted to enjoy themselves. Often that spilled over into drinking and fighting. One visitor, Edward Markham, was told that 'Some Sunday's 300 Men, from Thirty Whalers, have been on shore with their ladies and many a Row takes place.' The missionaries used to call the town 'Hell' (as opposed to 'Heaven', across the bay in Paihia) and later it was sometimes referred to as the 'hellhole of the Pacific'.

Missionaries, printers and schoolteachers

Samuel Marsden arrived with a group of missionaries from the Church Missionary Society (CMS) on 22 December 1814. He was English-born, but had been working in Australia. The CMS was established in 1799 with the aim of spreading Christianity around the world. Marsden thought that missionaries should be practical people with useful skills, which they could teach as well as sharing the **gospel**, so he chose Thomas Kendall (a teacher), William Hall (a carpenter) and John King (a rope maker).

On Christmas Day, Marsden preached a sermon on the beach at Oihi, below Rangihoua pā, where the first CMS mission station was set up under the protection of the Ngāpuhi leader Ruatara. This was where the CMS workers lived with their families, but it was isolated and the land was steep and no good for farming.

On 6 July 1815, Kendall recorded in his journal how he and Hall had been 'over the bay to Whitangi' to buy 50 acres of flat, fertile land there, it 'being the most eligible spot in the Bay of Islands for settlement'. The price was five

Augustus Earle

Other early visitors to New Zealand wrote about and sketched their travels. Their journals, diaries and letters tell us a lot about this period of history. They made up their own spellings for place names, because a written Māori language was still being developed. The London-born travel artist Augustus Earle (1793–1838) had already painted his way across the world when he was (as he tells us) 'wafted into the Great Pacific Ocean' in October 1827. In his *Narrative of a residence in New Zealand*, he describes how he sailed from Sydney to the Hokianga, and travelled by canoe and on foot to the Bay of Islands, painting the bush, beaches and waterfalls, houses and people along the way. He visited Koraradika (Kororāreka), Marsden Vale (Paihia) and Kiddy Kiddy (Kerikeri). Once, he camped at Wy-tanghe (Waitangi): 'No canoe being in sight, and we being too distant to make signals to our brig, we had to pass another night in bivouac on a part of the beach called Wy-tanghe; and as it did not rain, we slept pretty comfortably.'

Earle later joined Charles Darwin's ship the *Beagle*, but he fell sick in South America so never made it back to New Zealand.

Often Earle put himself in his paintings; here he depicts a meeting with the chief Hongi Hika.

axes, but the Ngātipou leader Waraki was hesitant about closing the deal. It was 'good for a few white people to live at New Zealand,' he said, 'but not for so many'.

Two convict workmen helped to build a house, and William Hall moved in with his wife Dinah, son and daughter (also called Dinah, and the first European baby girl to be born here). 'Wythangee is the garden of New Zealand,' he wrote enthusiastically. 'I have only been here four months and we have almost every useful kitchen vegetable in the highest state of perfection.' They didn't stay there long. Hall and his wife were injured when their house was attacked by a **taua muru**. The house was taken down and rebuilt at Rangihoua, but Hall kept tending his garden for several more years, until he left the country. No trace of the house remains, but it was probably near what is now called Hall's Gully.

Present-day Russell.

EARLY MEETINGS 11

Te ao Māori: Māori world view

Māori had (and still have) their own way of seeing, experiencing and interpreting the natural world (te taha kikokiko) and the spiritual world (te taha wairua). The Māori world view includes concepts such as whakapapa (genealogies and relationships), tapu (sacredness), mauri (life force), mana (power or authority), tika (justice) and tiaki (guardianship). Every living thing is thought to be inter-connected and related.

Some of the early European arrivals, such as missionary Thomas Kendall, made an effort to understand Māori society, customs, values and beliefs. Kendall took the Ngāpuhi leaders Hongi Hika and Waikato to England in 1820 and helped to produce the first Māori dictionary. (Māori had no written language, but they had a rich tradition of songs, poetry, proverbs, legends and speech making.)

However, this was not always the case, and differences between Māori and European ways of viewing the world led to misunderstandings and clashes of perspectives.

Marsden Cross was unveiled in March 1907 to commemorate the service taken at Rangihoua by Samuel Marsden in 1814.

Samuel Marsden's first service (Christmas Day 1814), from an illustration by Russell Clark to commemorate the 150th anniversary in 1964.

Samuel Marsden still thought of Waitangi as a possible site for a mission station. On 5 August 1823, he wrote in his journal about visiting there. 'The land is very good and the situation beautiful. We had some conversation with the inhabitants . . . but could come to no arrangements with them as the principal chiefs were absent at the wars.' CMS mission stations were set up instead at Kerikeri, Paihia (sometimes called Marsden Vale) and Waimate. Mission schools taught Māori children and adults to read and write.

Printers such as William Colenso began producing books, pamphlets and Bibles in English and Māori. In 1838, French bishop Jean-Baptiste Pompallier arrived at Hokianga with some Catholic missionaries and soon set up a tannery, printery and bookbindery in Kororāreka.

James Busby, man o' war with no guns

In 1831, the French naval ship *La Favorite* arrived in the Bay. A group of 13 Ngāpuhi leaders, worried about the intentions of the French, met at Kororipō pā and sent a letter to England's King William IV, asking for his protection both against 'the tribe of Marion' (the French) and against the lawless behaviour of some of the new settlers. This was one of the factors that led to the appointment of James Busby as British **Resident** in 1833. Busby's role was to try to keep law and order, but without army, police or any other power to back up his position he was soon being described as a '**man o' war** with no guns'.

Born in Scotland, James Busby (1802–1871) had emigrated to Australia with his family in 1824. He bought the land at Waitangi from William Hall when they met in Sydney. Once they had arrived in New Zealand, he and his wife Agnes stayed with one of the missionary families until their own house was ready.

> *Jan 1834: Monday, 27. Mr. and Mrs. Busby removed to their residence at Waitangi, and I had the pleasure of again possessing my Study, which had been occupied by them for these many months past.*
> **Journal of Henry Williams, CMS missionary in Paihia**

The house, **prefabricated** in Australia and shipped across in two stages, was smaller than he wanted, but the original plans had been scaled back to save money. It had only two rooms, a wide hall and a front verandah, with a separate block for the kitchen and servants quarters. A lean-to at the back and more rooms on the sides were added later.

James bought more land and drew up plans for a township, to be called Victoria. The new settlement was never built, but Busby was pleased with his garden, planted with fruit trees and grapevines, and wrote in 1839 that 'Waitangi is looking very beautiful'. He kept bees and was the first person to make wine in New Zealand. Visiting French naval officers were pleased and impressed; one presented him with wineglasses, and Jules Dumont d'Urville praised the results as 'a light wine, very sparkling and delicious to taste'. Another visitor described the house as a 'pretty neat, and hospitable Mansion embodied in a grove of trees and shrubs, with flowers sending forth a rich fragrance'.

James Busby, painted in 1832 by Richard Read.

AGNES BUSBY

Agnes Busby (c1800–1889) was always busy, cooking and cleaning — often without servants — and entertaining visitors. She had six children in nine years: John, Sarah, James, George, William and Agnes. (Not all of them survived to adulthood.)

Agnes was present for the signing of the Treaty of Waitangi, and the opening of the meeting house at Te Tii in 1881. She came back to live in Waitangi after James Busby's death in 1871, saying, 'The longer I live, the more I miss him here at Waitangi where no one else can fill his place.' She is buried in the churchyard of St Paul's Church at Paihia.

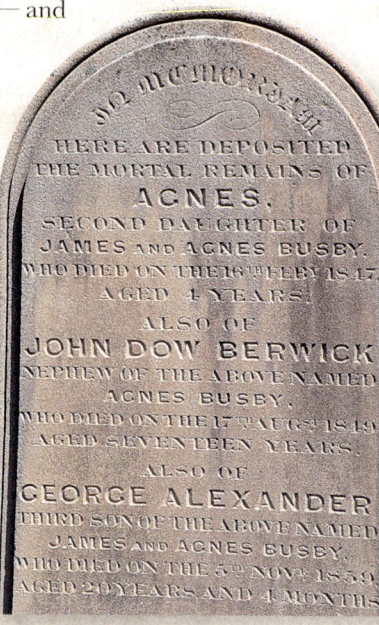

Busby family gravestone at Paihia.

SARAH BUSBY

Sarah, Agnes's second child, was born in 1835 in the main bedroom of the Treaty House. When she was three months old, a fight broke out between two groups of Māori who had come to discuss a land dispute. One group fired muskets at the others, who ran inside the house for protection. Some pulled sheets off the beds to bandage their wounds. Agnes grabbed her little boy, John, but the baby's cradle was empty. Then Agnes saw that one of the men had already picked Sarah up to keep her safe and was sheltering her under his cloak.

Sarah was the oldest daughter and must often have helped her mother. The Reverend William Cotton stayed with the Busby family when Sarah was nine. He wrote, 'Sarah B acting as nursemaid, sweeping the room — she does capitally, entering into all that is to be done, taking care of the baby — as tho' she understood it all.'

At age 19, Sarah married John William Williams (son of the Reverend Henry Williams and his wife Marianne) and they had 11 children — eight boys and three girls. They lived at Pakaraka (inland from Waitangi), then Napier. Sarah died in Gisborne in 1913.

This postcard depicts the 1834 ceremony at which the northern leaders chose the first national flag of New Zealand.

1834: Choosing a national flag

Ocean-going ships had to identify the country they came from by carrying a register (a certificate of ownership) and displaying their country's flag. New Zealand was still an independent country — not a British **colony** — and ships built here had no register and no flag to sail under, which meant that the ship and its cargo could be seized at a foreign port. This happened to a ship from the Hokianga, which was seized in Sydney in 1830.

A national flag was needed, so James Busby called a meeting of 25 northern rangatira (or leaders) and their followers. On 20 March 1834, they met on the lawn at Waitangi, in front of the Busbys' new house. The rangatira chose from three possible designs and the majority voted for 'Te Kara', which featured a large red St George's Cross and a smaller cross with four white stars. This became known as the Flag of the United Tribes of New Zealand.

After the Treaty was signed in 1840, the Union Jack became New Zealand's national flag. It was replaced in turn by today's national flag, introduced by Act of Parliament in 1902.

1835: He Wakaputanga o te Rangatiratanga o Nu Tīrene (A Declaration of the Independence of New Zealand)

An eccentric Frenchman called Baron Charles de Thierry was rumoured to be on the way to New Zealand, intending to create a separate colony at Hokianga with himself as sovereign chief. James Busby, worried this might lead to fighting and unrest, called another meeting. On 28 October 1835, 34 northern leaders signed 'A Declaration of the Independence of New Zealand' (He Wakaputanga o te Rangatiratanga o Nu Tīreni), in which they thanked King William IV for acknowledging their flag, but also asked him to be the 'parent' and 'protector' of their nation. They called themselves Heads of the **Confederation** of the United Tribes of New Zealand (Te Whakaminenga o ngā hapū o Nu Tīreni) and declared the country to be an independent state.

These developments (Te Kara and He Wakaputanga) both marked an effort by Māori to create a unified voice and to assert their sovereignty.

De Thierry did arrive at Hokianga in 1837, but his proposed French colony came to nothing. He tried other ways to make a living, such as goldmining, teaching French and music, piano tuning and flax processing, and died in Auckland in 1864.

Later a French ship, the *Comte de Paris*, brought settlers to establish a French colony on Banks Peninsula in the South Island. The French naval corvette *L'Aube* sailed ahead of it and reached the Bay of Islands in July 1840, but by then Hobson had already claimed the whole country, including

This 1838 print shows sailors from the French vessel *Venus* repairing a small craft under the gaze of Māori. In the background is the Kororāreka waterfront.

Documents of the 1835 Declaration of Independence.

EARLY MEETINGS 15

1835: Charles Darwin's visit

The English naturalist Charles Darwin, on board HMS *Beagle*, arrived in the Bay of Islands from Tahiti in December 1835. During his stay, Darwin inspected some large kauri trees and collected a few specimens. He and the ship's captain, Robert FitzRoy, also donated some money to help build Christ Church in Kororāreka. By now Darwin had been at sea for four years; he was grumpy and critical of nearly everything apart from the mission station at Waimate, because it reminded him of an English farm-house, 'placed there as if by an enchanter's wand'.

Charles Darwin collected this red gurnard during his 1835 visit to the Bay of Islands; it is now kept in a museum in Cambridge, England.

the South Island, for the British **Crown**. The French emigrants still landed at Akaroa, where you can see French place names and traces of French colonial architecture.

The hui and signing of the Treaty (Te Tiriti)

The British remained worried that another country, especially France or the United States, might try to take over New Zealand, and they were also concerned about possible land-buying practices of the newly formed New Zealand Company, which had already sent their representatives, on board the *Tory*, to buy and survey land for emigrants. They appointed Captain William Hobson as lieutenant-governor and sent him to make a treaty with the Māori leaders.

Captain Hobson arrived from Sydney on the HMS *Herald* on 29 January 1840, with an English draft of the Treaty that still had to be finished and translated. (Some of the rangatira knew English, but not all of them, and Hobson did not speak the Māori language.) James Busby worked on the text of the Treaty, and Henry Williams translated it into the Māori language with the help of his son Edward. The translation (Te Tiriti) would lead to later misunderstandings and controversy over differences between the Māori and the English texts, especially regarding the English words 'sovereignty' and 'possession' and the Māori words 'kāwanatanga' and 'te tino rangatiratanga'.

The rangatira were invited to attend a meeting on 5 February 1840 at Waitangi. That morning, Captain Hobson and Captain Nias, the commander of the *Herald*, were rowed ashore to the beach and walked up the track to James Busby's house. In front of the house, sailors had put up a huge tent, made of sails and decorated with flags. A table covered with the Union Jack stood on a raised platform.

There were many people present: Māori, missionaries, sailors and officers from the *Herald* and other ships, and

Captain Hobson is rowed ashore at the 1940 re-enactment of these events.

16 WAITANGI DAY

Diary entry for 5 February 1840 of Henry Comber, one of several naval officers who attended the signing.

local settlers and residents, and some of them, like William Colenso, have left eyewitness descriptions of what happened next. Midshipman Henry Comber, from the *Herald*, also described the scene in his journal:

> *All our officers went to make a show, and about 10 AM we assembled to the number of 6 or 7 hundred, about 1/3 of whom were Europeans, the rest Natives. His Excellency Captain Hobson took his station on a stage, Accompanied by Captain Nias, and his officers, all the Missionaries, The French Bishop and his Priests, and some few gentlemen.*

With Henry Williams acting as translator, there were heated discussions about the proposed Treaty and some moments of humour. Many Māori spoke against it, telling Hobson to get back in his ship and sail away again. Only a few seemed in favour. Hobson proposed to meet again in two days' time, but by the next morning, stores of food were running low and some of the rangatira were already starting to depart. Hobson left the *Herald* in such a rush that he didn't have time to put on his naval uniform, and wore his plumed hat with ordinary clothes. He declared that this was not a proper meeting, so he could not accept more discussion, only signatures. Led by the Ngāpuhi leader Heke Pokai (also known as Hone Heke), about 40 rangatira signed the document.

The signing of the Treaty of Waitangi, painted by Marcus King. Reconstructions like these often show Hobson in full naval uniform at the signing, but this wasn't the case.

'He iwi tahi tātou'

'He iwi tahi tātou', often translated as 'we are now one people', is what Lieutenant-Governor Hobson said to each rangatira who signed the Treaty (Te Tiriti). In later years, some Māori would object to the implied suggestion that Pākehā society would swallow up Māori identity. However, there are other possible translations. **Anthropologist** Dame Joan Metge says that in 1840 these words could have meant 'We two people together make a nation'. Another translation could be 'We many peoples together make one nation'.

Māori women sign Te Tiriti

Thirteen high-ranking Māori women signed Te Tiriti (the Treaty), including ancestors of Dame Whina Cooper and Princess Te Puea Herangi. Some signed at Waitangi on 6 February; others signed elsewhere. It is possible that more Māori women might have signed if their leadership and mana had been recognised by some of the Pākehā men who were collecting signatures. Kahe Te Rau-o-te-Rangi, of Ngāti Toa and Ngāti Mutunga descent, signed Te Tiriti on 29 April 1840 at Port Nicholson (Wellington). She lived on Kāpiti Island with her Pākehā husband, an ex-whaler, and sailed with him on his trading expeditions. She was seen as a leader of mana and was famous for swimming from Kāpiti to the mainland with her baby Ripeka on her back to warn of an impending attack. Rangi Topeora, of Ngāti Toa and Ngāti Raukawa, was a musician and a composer of waiata, famous for her leadership, her warlike deeds and her efforts at making peace. She signed Henry Williams' copy of the Treaty on 14 May 1840.

Portrait of Rangi Topeora taken by an unknown photographer in about 1840.

Over the next few months, the Treaty was copied out and taken around the country, starting with Waimate and Mangungu. About 500 signatures were gathered on nine different sheets, with the majority of the Māori leaders signing Te Tiriti, the Māori language version. Some rangatira signed their names; others put a cross or drew the pattern of their moko.

Okiato, New Zealand's first capital

For his new capital, Hobson chose Okiato, a sheltered spot with a jetty where an American named James Clendon ran a trading post. Hobson bought the land, house and buildings, moved his official residence there, and had plans drawn up for a new town, to be called Russell, but it was never built. The site was abandoned when the capital was moved to Auckland in February 1841. Kororāreka was later renamed Russell — the name it is known by today — and Okiato (sometimes called Old Russell) has gone back to its original name.

Hone Heke, the flagpole and the burning of Kororāreka

Hone Heke was the first to sign Te Tiriti o Waitangi (his signature now appears fourth as other leaders signed above him). Later he became critical of the British Government. Trade at Kororāreka had dropped off because of new customs duties, and the Bay of Islands became a neglected backwater while Auckland grew busier and bigger. Hone Heke felt disillusioned about the promises that had been made and his discontent centred on the flagpole. This had been a gift from Hone Heke to James Busby, but Hobson had since moved it from Waitangi to Maiki Hill at Kororāreka and replaced the Flag of the United Tribes of New Zealand with the Union Jack.

In July 1844, Hone Heke and his followers cut down the flagpole to show their opposition to the Union Jack and what it symbolised. Each time the flagpole was put up, they cut it down again, even when it was partly sheathed in iron and protected by guards. A reward of £100 was announced for the capture of Hone Heke, and he responded by offering a similar reward for the capture of Governor Fitzroy. The fourth and final time that the flagpole was cut down was on 11 March 1845, when Hone Heke launched an attack on Kororāreka and most of the town burnt to the ground. Fighting between British and Ngāpuhi forces continued over 1845–46 in what is now called the Northern War.

Many years later, Henry Kemp, looking back on these events, wrote that Hone Heke's real object was not to attack Kororāreka, but to free his people and 'to make for himself the name of liberator and champion of their rights and liberties'.

This 1908 painting shows Hone Heke felling the flagpole.

Hariata (Harriet) Rongo

Hariata (Harriet) Rongo was the daughter of Ngāpuhi leader Hongi Hika. She lived for some years with the family of CMS missionary James Kemp and married Hone Heke in the Kerikeri chapel in May 1837. On display at Kemp House (see page 55) is the writing slate that she used at the mission school.

CHAPTER 2

WHAT HAPPENED NEXT?

1840–1890: The first 50 years of the Treaty

For many years, the Treaty was ignored, disregarded or even rejected by Pākehā, and the date of 6 February went unmarked. In 1877, Chief Justice James Prendergast ruled in a Māori land case that the Treaty was 'worthless' and a 'legal nullity', which meant that it had no legal standing and the government didn't need to take it into account.

But Māori never forgot the importance of the Treaty, and referred back to it constantly in their attempts to solve **grievances**, especially relating to land. Māori lost vast areas of land as a result of the 1840s–1870s New Zealand Wars, and the establishment of the Native Land Court in 1865. As well as presenting hundreds of petitions to Parliament, several delegations of Māori (including the second Māori King, Tāwhiao) travelled to England to present petitions in person to Queen Victoria, and later to King George V, but they were told to take them back to their own government.

The Kingitanga or Māori King movement began with the first Māori King, Potatau Te Wherowhero, crowned in 1858. The New Zealand Parliament included four Māori MPs from 1868, but they held little power. The Māori Parliament, Kotahitanga mo te Tiriti o Waitangi, was formed at a meeting in Waitangi in 1892 and met at various places over the next decade, including at the Waitangi Treaty Hall, to consider Māori needs and present them to Parliament in Wellington.

1881: Te Tii marae

Te Tii marae sits on the Paihia side of the Waitangi River and includes the site where the Māori rangatira met on the night of 5 February 1840 to discuss the Treaty. In April 1875, a hall was erected for a wedding, and a decision was made to name it Te Tiriti o Waitangi ('The Treaty of Waitangi'). It was visited by the governor, Lord Normanby, the following year, but was soon to be replaced by a new, larger building.

On 23 March 1881, 41 years after the signing of the Treaty, this new meeting house was opened by the Native Minister, William Rolleston. The building (also called the

Te Tii marae.

This 1880 photograph of Te Tii marae shows the meeting house Te Tiriti o Waitangi (foreground) and the Waitangi Treaty memorial (right of meeting house). A Māori petition to Queen Victoria included the words 'In this year, 1881, we, O the Queen, built a House of Assembly at the Bay of Islands, and the great symbol therein is a Stone memorial, on which has been engraved the articles of the Treaty of Waitangi, so that eyes may look thereon from year to year.'

Waitangi Treaty Hall) would host many **hui** over the next decades, where Māori could discuss Treaty and other issues that concerned them. Ngāpuhi had raised £1000 to pay for its construction and for the opening celebrations; the stack of food provided was 'a solid wall of potato kits, about three feet high and three feet wide, extending for nearly a quarter of a mile', topped by 500 dried sharks, with 200 pigs waiting nearby. A memorial displaying the Māori text of Te Tiriti o Waitangi was also erected at this time. The governor, Sir Arthur Gordon, had been invited to unveil it and Māori were disappointed when he didn't come.

This memorial still stands, but the hall was blown down by a storm in 1917, and the Māori Women's League (now the Māori Women's Welfare League) built a replacement. The women took charge of the project, partly because so many local men had died in the First World War or the 'flu epidemic. The new hall contained a memorial to Māori soldiers who served in the war; it was opened on 29 March 1922 by Prime Minister William Massey, who used the table that had served in the original Treaty signing. Te Tii marae still plays an important part in Waitangi Day celebrations. Meetings and debates are held there on 5 February, mirroring the discussions that took place on 5 February 1840.

1890: The fiftieth anniversary

In 1890, the nation celebrated its fiftieth anniversary. Jubilee events in Auckland included bands and parades, a regatta, a swimming carnival, a meeting at the Takapuna racecourse, and fireworks set off from a ferry in the harbour. But the celebrations began on 29 January, and it was this date (marking Captain Hobson's arrival in the Bay of Islands), not 6 February (the signing of the Treaty), that the Government identified as 'the fiftieth anniversary of the colony' when it awarded a public holiday.

> *Official records have been carefully looked into, the dust of years has been shaken off 'Gazettes' and everything possible has been done to settle the question once and for all. In the minds of those possessed of any information on the subject there never could have been a doubt as to the date.*
> — **Auckland Star, 17 January 1890**

For several more decades, 29 January would be viewed as New Zealand's anniversary day, but the Treaty, overlooked by Pākehā, remained significant to Māori. Āpirana Ngata wrote in his book *The Treaty of Waitangi*, published in 1922: 'At the present time the Treaty is widely discussed on all maraes. It is on the lips of the humble and the great, of the ignorant and of the thoughtful.'

Occasionally, the date of the Treaty signing was more widely recognised. On 6 February 1928, thousands of people listened in to a radio broadcast of a Māori concert party from Wanganui and several speeches, including one by the prime minister, Gordon Coates, who paid tribute to the Māori soldiers who had served in the First World War. Radio was still in its early days, and the full programme could only be broadcast to Christchurch, Auckland and Dunedin once darkness fell and reception became clearer.

The Busbys' house falls into disrepair

The Busbys had remained at Waitangi, although James Busby no longer held the position of Resident. During the Northern War in 1845–46, the family left to avoid the fighting; the British Army's 58th Regiment camped in the grounds and the officers lived in the house.

James Busby made a number of trips overseas, trying to raise money to pay his debts and to settle land claims, and died in England after an eye operation in 1871. His sons John and William looked after the property, and later Agnes sold

This cap badge of a soldier of the 58th Regiment was found in about 1920 on the beach at Te Wahapu, near Russell.

WHAT HAPPENED NEXT?

James Busby's house in 1903.

it to a local farmer; at one stage the house served as a shearing shed and a shelter for sheep. Broken glass in the windows was replaced with sacking, the roof began leaking and the ceilings sagged. Some owners made a few repairs, and one divided up the land into smaller sections and tried to sell them off for a township called Raurimu, but like James Busby's Victoria (page 12), this didn't work. There was talk of buying the land for a national memorial, but the government couldn't afford it.

The Bledisloe gift

Lord Bledisloe was the fourth governor-general of New Zealand. In February 1932, he and his wife came to the Bay of Islands on holiday. They were so impressed with the beauty of Waitangi and its importance as a historical site that they decided to buy the Treaty House and grounds (1000 acres in all) from its current owner, Mr Hewin, and present them as a gift to the nation. Their plan was announced to the public in May 1932. (Six months later they made a further gift of another 1350 acres.)

> 'Waitangi' is a household word in New Zealand, and every school child knows about the Treaty, but it required the genius of his Excellency the Governor-General and the Lady Bledisloe to see the real significance of the spot where that famous document was signed.
> — *Auckland Star*, 11 May 1932

Before the house could be formally handed over to the nation in 1934, it needed a lot of restoration work. Some money was raised by using wood from the house to make and sell souvenirs such as candlesticks, paper knives, rulers, napkin rings and paper weights. The garden, overgrown and uncared for, also needed attention. The Waitangi River bridge — connecting Waitangi with Paihia — was hurriedly completed, and motorists were warned that the roads were narrow and they would have to drive carefully.

Lord and Lady Bledisloe standing with a gathering of Māori.

Lord Bledisloe (1867–1958)

Charles Bathurst was an English lawyer and Member of Parliament. As Lord Bledisloe, he was governor-general of New Zealand during the Depression years of 1930–35. When public servants had their salaries cut, he asked for his salary to be reduced as well; this was just one of the reasons why he and his wife were so respected and well liked. Lord Bledisloe gave his name to Mt Bledisloe, a hill providing a good viewpoint 3 km from Waitangi, and to the Bledisloe Cup (in size, the biggest trophy in world rugby), which he donated in 1931 for a test rugby competition between the All Blacks and the Wallabies.

View from Mt Bledisloe looking towards Waitangi River bridge, with Waitangi on the left and Te Tii marae on the right of the bridge.

Lord and Lady Bledisloe's purchase of the Waitangi National Reserve was a generous and inspired gift that raised awareness of the site and its significance amongst Pākehā New Zealanders.

1934: Big celebrations at Waitangi

In February 1934, people headed towards Waitangi from all parts of the country. The prime minister came, as did the governor-general and his wife. About 50 MPs, their wives and families boarded a special 'Parliamentary train', which stopped at Opua wharf.

Hundreds of Māori also made their way north by train. In Auckland, they filled the streets and attracted curious stares from city dwellers, who didn't often come in contact with Māori. (Three-quarters of the Māori population were still living in rural areas.) At the railway station, some Māori who spoke little English could not communicate easily with

Taking care of the grounds

The Waitangi National Trust Board was set up by an Act of Parliament in 1932 to administer the Waitangi Treaty Grounds and associated lands. The board included representatives of the government and of families (Māori and Pākehā) who had a connection with the signing of the Treaty. It first met on 30 March 1933. Today's board is still made up of descendants and representatives of people directly associated with the Treaty and the grounds.

Waitangi National Trust Board members meeting in the 1930s.

the ticket-sellers, but it was taken for granted that they wanted tickets to Opua.

This was the largest gathering of Māori for many years. Visitors were welcomed from Whakatāne and Ruatoki, Opōtiki and the East Coast, Rotorua and Taupō, Taranaki, Hawke's Bay and Waikato. The site was a bustle of activity, with 75 carpenters busy at work. A grandstand was built for the official party and there were eight large marquees and many smaller tents. Haka and dance groups spent hours practising. Sam Maoha, the kai haona, (official crier) broadcast announcements over a megaphone that could be heard in Paihia.

Feeding so many people, day after day, was a huge challenge. Stores of food included:

- 1500 sacks of potatoes
- 62 bullocks and 60 pigs
- six tons of sugar
- 100 sacks of cabbages
- several chests of tea
- thousands of loaves of bread

Vegetables were cooked in steamers, meat was roasted in outdoor ovens, and pastries and puddings were baked in the cookhouse. The food was carried on a small wooden railway to the dining marquees, where rows of benches could each fit 54 people, and 650 in total could eat at each sitting. An overnight storm blew down some of the tents, but Sir Āpirana Ngata said there would be no cancellations because of the weather. The celebrations 'must go on, wet or fine, wind or rain'.

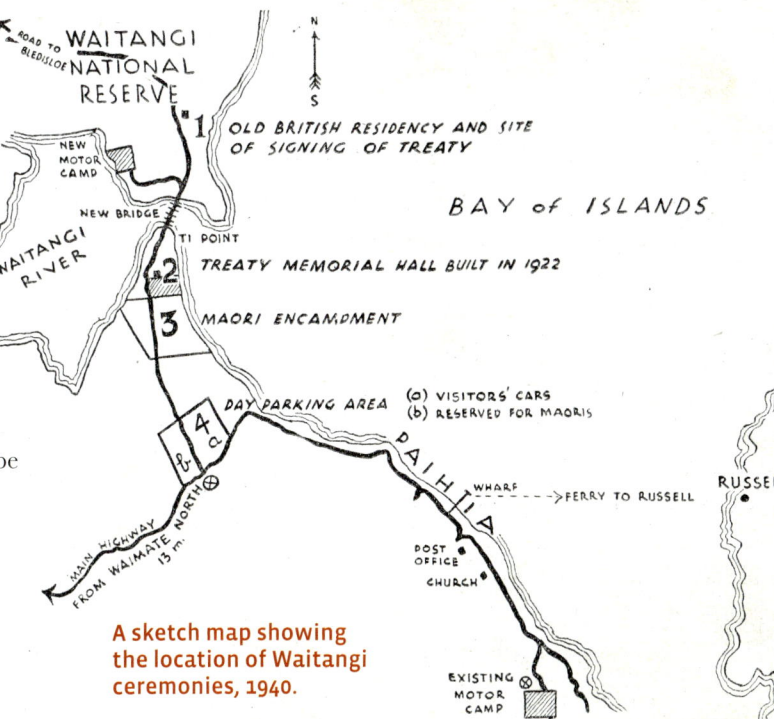

A sketch map showing the location of Waitangi ceremonies, 1940.

Hui at Waitangi to celebrate the gift of property where the Treaty of Waitangi was signed, 1934. View over tents and marquees to Treaty House in the trees beyond the bridge. Te Tii marae in foreground.

WAITANGI DAY

Sunday, 4 February, was brilliantly fine and Bishop Frederick Bennett, the first Māori bishop of Aotearoa, led the church service. Two warships were anchored in the bay, ferries criss-crossed the water, and over 1200 motor cars clogged the roads. At 2.30 p.m. on Monday, 5 February, Lord and Lady Bledisloe arrived to loud cheers from thousands of spectators. Other special guests included a party of Rarotongan ariki (chiefs) and their families, and representatives of old Waitangi families such as the Williams, Kemps and Busbys. Also present was Korokī, in his first major public appearance as the fifth Māori King, having just taken over from his father, Te Rata.

On Tuesday, 6 February, Lord Bledisloe released the Union Jack from the new mast. He officially inspected the residency and dedicated the foundation stone, or carved threshold, of the new meeting house. He had written a prayer, 'for the faithful observance of the Treaty of Waitangi', which was read out by the bishop; this is called the Bledisloe Prayer, and it is still sometimes used.

The spectacular turnout for the ceremonies in 1934 included these Rarotongan princesses.

Getting everyone back home took more organisation. Extra trains were put on for many Māori who were returning south. Some had to sleep in their carriages at Auckland until their connecting trains were ready.

Āpirana Ngata leading a haka in front of the meeting house at the 1940 centennial celebrations at Waitangi.

Sir Āpirana Turupa Ngata (1874–1950)

Born on the East Coast, the eldest of 15 children in a Ngāti Porou family, Āpirana Ngata was educated at Waiomatatini Native School and Te Aute College. He went on to study law and became the first Māori to graduate from a New Zealand university. He was travelling secretary for the Young Māori Party and was a Member of Parliament for nearly 40 years. In 1927, he was knighted for his services to the Māori people, especially relating to the recruitment of Māori for war service, Māori land development schemes, and his support for Māori art, language and culture. In 1934, he was Minister of Native Affairs (as the Minister of Māori Affairs was called then). Later he helped to organise the 1940 centennial celebrations and the building of the **whare rūnanga** at Waitangi. Today his picture is on the front of the New Zealand $50 note.

WHAT HAPPENED NEXT? **25**

Members of Ngāti Tūwharetoa perform the peruperu, acknowledging the gift of Waitangi land to the nation by Lord Bledisloe, on 6 February 1934.

Waitangi from the air

Some people got to see Waitangi from the air — an unusual experience in those days. Sir Charles Kingsford-Smith, the famous Australian aviator, took off from Māngere in his Fokker monoplane, the *Southern Cross*, on the morning of 5 February 1934. His passengers included a blind father with his eight-year-old son, who brought two bottles of ginger beer and a bag of fruit for the journey. The wheels of the plane were touching the ground at Waitangi when Sir Charles decided that there wasn't enough room to land; he took off again, dropping overboard some mail. The following day he repeated the trip with different passengers. This time he did land, and the newspaper reported that 'hordes of people temporarily deserted the camp to inspect the famous machine'.

A few lucky people saw this aerial view of the Waitangi celebrations.

In 1928, crowds flocked to Wigram Airfield in Christchurch to see the arrival of Kingsford-Smith's *Southern Cross*.

1940: The New Zealand Centennial

The Bledisloe gift had made people more aware of the importance of Waitangi, and the Treaty House was open to a steady stream of visitors; but 6 February wasn't yet seen as a significant date. From 1933, an annual church service and dinner took place in London for New Zealand Day, but the date chosen for the first such occasion (when a wreath was also laid on James Busby's grave in a London cemetery) was 8 February, marking the gun salute fired from the *Herald* in honour of the successful completion of Captain Hobson's mission. A newspaper report on the 1939 London dinner added that 'in the Dominion itself the day is not celebrated in any special way'.

The year 1940 marked the New Zealand Centennial. Waitangi was referred to as 'the cradle of New Zealand's history', but overall more attention seemed to be paid to 100 years of European progress and the achievements of the early pioneers. Around the country there were pageants, parades and unveilings of memorials. Despite the start of the Second World War, thousands of people still flocked to the Centennial Exhibition at Rongotai in Wellington from November 1939 to May 1940.

Re-enacting history

On 6 February 1940, crowds of spectators at Waitangi watched actors re-enact a telescoped version of the events of a century before. Out in the bay, tattooed warriors paddled war canoes. Captain Hobson, Captain Nias and other officers of the *Herald*, dressed in old-fashioned uniforms, were rowed ashore by sailors and met at the beach by a group of early settlers (*see* photo page 15). Māori warriors guided them up the Nias Track to the Treaty House, where the discussions over the Treaty were played out, with the Māori leaders speaking for or against it until finally, led by Hone Heke, they signed or put their marks on the sheet of paper, Hobson declared 'He iwi tahi tātou', and the Union Jack was raised.

A 1940 Centennial Exhibition certificate.

Centennial stamps, 1940.

WHAT HAPPENED NEXT? 27

A 1935 Waitangi Crown showing Tamati Waka Nene shaking hands with Captain William Hobson.

The **waka taua** (war canoe) *Ngātokimatawhaorua* was launched and Viscount Galway, the governor-general, officially opened the whare rūnanga. The four Māori MPs gave speeches. Memorials to William Hobson, James Busby, and the Māori leaders who signed the Treaty (Te Tiriti) were unveiled. Guests included descendants of Māori rangatira such as Hone Heke, Kawiti and Patuone, and of the Busby,

Characters dress as pioneer ladies for the Treaty signing re-enactment of 1940.

Williams and other families. However, not everyone thought it was an occasion to celebrate. Taranaki and Waikato leaders, including King Korokī and Te Puea Herangi, did not come to Waitangi.

Waka taua

The waka taua *Ngātokimatawhaorua* was built for the 1940 celebrations and named after Kupe's canoe. In Māori tradition, Kupe first came to New Zealand in the canoe *Matawhaorua*. When he returned to Hawaiki, that canoe was adzed again and renamed ('Ngātoki' means 'the adzes'), and Nukutāwhiti brought it back to New Zealand.

Ngātokimatawhaorua — often known as *Ngātoki* — was made from three ancient kauri trees: one for the central section, one for the bow and stern, and one for raising the sides above water level. The trees were partly hollowed out, soaked in water at Waipapa Landing for three months, and dried for three months before being carved. Today *Ngātoki* is launched every year as part of the Waitangi Day celebrations.

Ngātokimatawhaorua . . .
- took two-and-a-half years to build
- measures 35.7 metres long
- weighs 12 tonnes
- can take 40 paddlers each side, plus another 40 people sitting in the middle
- can travel at 13 knots (25 km/h).

The Ngāpuhi waka taua (war canoe) Ngātokimatawhaorua, built for the 1940 centennial, at Waitangi Day 2002.

WAITANGI DAY

Māori women and men welcome the soldiers outside the meeting house.

THE MĀORI BATTALION

A special appearance was put in by 500 members of the 28th (Māori) Battalion, chosen to represent tribes from all over New Zealand. The battalion had only been in training for a week when the soldiers left the Palmerston North showgrounds early in the morning of 4 February 1940. They travelled to Auckland and then to Opua by train, arriving at 5 a.m. the following day. From there, a fleet of small boats took them to Waitangi for a pōwhiri and welcoming ceremony. In reply to a haka, the soldiers performed their new marching song, 'Māori Battalion March to Victory'.

When the soldiers left to return to Palmerston North, the warriors in the waka taua farewelled them with a haka of encouragement. Their visit remains the only time that an army unit has paraded at Waitangi.

The Māori battalion march to their camp at Waitangi.

The Treaty on show

The 1940 celebrations at Waitangi included the first public display of the original Treaty documents. There are nine of these altogether.

- Eight are handwritten, one printed.
- Eight are in the Māori language, one (the Waikato-Manukau Treaty) in English.
- Two are on parchment (the Waitangi Treaty and the *Herald* sheet), the rest on paper.
- The original drafts in English and the Māori language have disappeared.

The documents weren't in perfect condition, but it was lucky they even existed. After being signed, they were kept in a small iron box in the government offices in Auckland. A records clerk, George Elliot, woke one morning in 1841 to see smoke billowing from that direction.

> *When I got to the building, one end was in flames. I saw that nothing could save the place. I at once tied my handkerchief over my face, got the door open and rushed into the room which the Colonial Secretary occupied. I could not see for smoke and the handkerchief both blinded and choked me. The room was small and I knew it so well I could put my hand on anything blindfolded. I at once went to the iron box, unlocked it and took out the Treaty of Waitangi and the seal of the colony and ran out again.*
> —*Auckland Star*, 17 February 1926

After that, the Treaty documents were stored in the colonial secretary's office, and moved to Wellington when the capital city shifted there. Copies of them were made in 1877. When Dr Thomas Hocken, a historian, found them in the basement of the Government Buildings in 1908, they had suffered water damage and rats had nibbled away at the edges of the parchment. (Parchment, a writing material made from goat or sheep skin, was often used for legal documents because it was tough and durable, but it also made a tasty snack for rats.)

The documents were repaired by being mounted on canvas or linen, but restoration techniques were limited and the starch paste used eventually caused more damage. More careful restoration work was carried out in the 1970s and 1980s. In 1991, the original documents went to the Constitution Room of National Archives in Wellington.

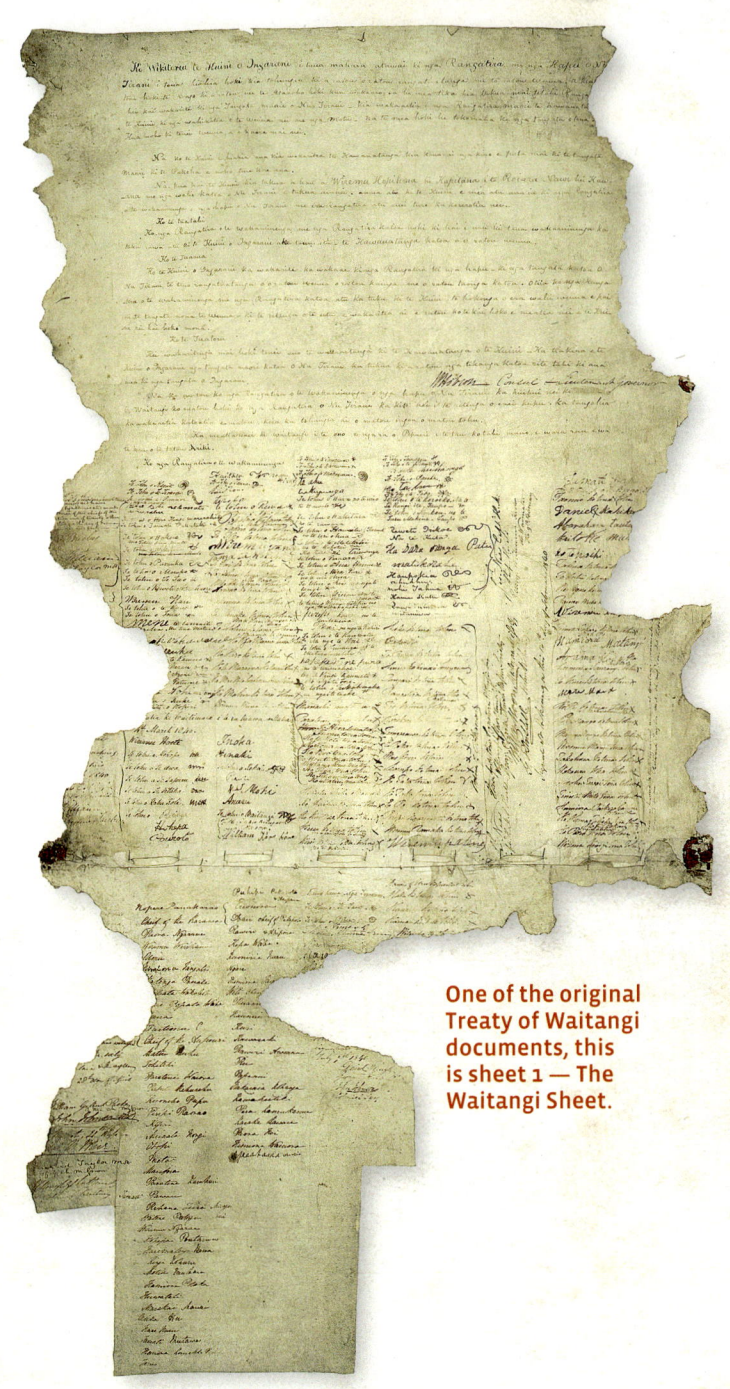

One of the original Treaty of Waitangi documents, this is sheet 1 — The Waitangi Sheet.

The Second World War

During the war, the army used the property and grounds at Waitangi. In 1941–42, people were worried about a possible Japanese invasion. Soldiers lived in huts in the Russell Domain, and officers moved into Pompallier House. Defences in the Bay of Islands included a coastal battery with gun emplacements at Waitata Point near Russell, a mine control station on Moturua Island, and a radar and coast-watching station at Cape Brett.

WAITANGI DAY

After 1940, the next significant celebration was not until 1947, when the Royal New Zealand Navy held a ceremony at the new flagpole and took over responsibility for maintaining it. From then on, an annual commemoration took place at Waitangi in the presence of the governor-general (and sometimes the prime minister), as well as other speakers, both Māori and Pākehā; the ceremony usually included both a naval salute and a Māori cultural performance.

The army buildings put up at Waitangi during the war were later used for school camps. These were unusual in the 1940s and schools needed the Education Department's permission to visit during term-time. The mess room was divided in half to make a common room at one end and sleeping quarters at the other, furnished with army bunks and straw mattresses.

The first school group came in 1946 from Kaitaia District High School. Footage from a film taken of their visit shows them driving in an old bus along dusty roads, walking around the Treaty Grounds, being rowed ashore at Marsden Cross, visiting Russell, swimming, and playing cricket.

Detonating mines at the entrance to the Bay of Islands, 1944. These had been laid as a precaution against possible Japanese invasion.

A few days later they headed home again. More school groups followed and other students came on day trips, but the school visit programme stopped after about 1950.

Royal New Zealand Navy on parade for Waitangi Day, 1947.

CHAPTER 3

CHANGE, PROTEST AND PROGRESS

1953: Queen Elizabeth comes to Waitangi

Members of the British royal family had paid visits to New Zealand since 1869. The visit by Queen Elizabeth II and her husband Philip, Duke of Edinburgh, caused huge excitement. Queen Elizabeth had only recently ascended the throne, and this was the first time a ruling monarch had come to New Zealand. Months of work went into sealing roads, painting buildings, planting flowers, and putting up flags and decorations all over the country. The royal couple arrived in Auckland on 23 December 1953, only a day before the terrible accident at Tangiwai when a bridge collapsed late on Christmas Eve, sending a packed train tumbling into the rushing water below and killing 151 of the 285 passengers and crew. The Queen ended her Christmas radio broadcast with a message of sympathy to all those affected by the tragedy.

Māori ceremonies were not seen as a priority by the government; the original royal itinerary allowed for only one Māori reception at Rotorua, and left out both Waitangi and Tūrangawaewae, the seat of the Māori King at Ngāruawāhia. This was disappointing to many Māori who felt that the Treaty, a document signed on Queen Victoria's behalf by Captain Hobson, was a **covenant** giving them a special link to the British monarchy, and

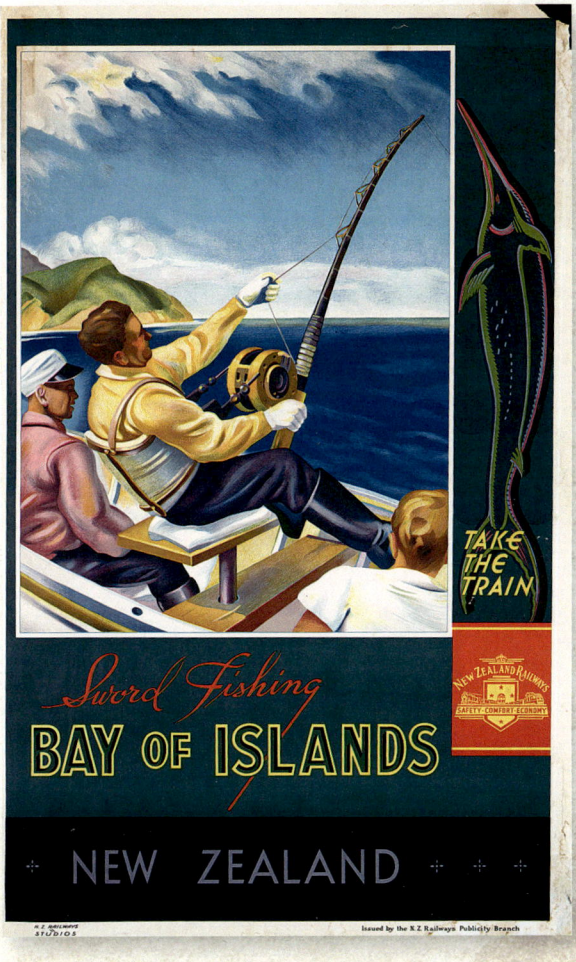

Tourism posters advertised New Zealand, including the Bay of Islands, as a sportsman's paradise.

to Queen Elizabeth as the great-great-granddaughter of Queen Victoria.

After protests from Māori leaders, the royals paid a one-hour visit to Waitangi on 28 December. (This was the first formal meeting between the monarch and the Māori people.) A three-minute stop was slotted in, at the last moment, for Tūrangawaewae.

Overall, the 1953 tour was a huge success. It was estimated that three out of four New Zealanders saw the royal couple at some stage, and their visit to Waitangi, even if only short, brought Waitangi back into public attention.

1963: THE ROYALS RETURN

On 6 February 1963, the Queen and Prince Philip sailed into the Bay of Islands on the royal yacht *Britannia*. Once again, thousands of people had turned out, and the Army provided field kitchens and over 200 eight-person tents for the Te Tii marae, but so many busloads of people kept arriving that they had to squeeze 12 into each tent.

The visit was seen as 'a day of splendid delight' and 'a memorable night of ceremony and pageant'. The royal couple met a number of 'eminent Māori' representing all the tribes of New Zealand. They looked round the Treaty House and had tea, served in the 'quiet little parlour' by the manager's wife, Mrs Lindsay. 'The Queen walked over to the table to get her tea as she likes it, with very little milk and no sugar, and she ate a piece of Mrs Lindsay's shortbread.' Both the Queen and the Duke signed the Visitors' Book.

> *The earth we stand on here is historic ground, as meaningful to our nation as, say, Runnymede or Gettysburg have been to others.*
> **Prime Minister Keith Holyoake, during the royal visit of 1963**

During a walk around the Treaty House grounds, the Duke noticed the shell of a battered old truck. This was *Te Rau Aroha* ('a gift of love'), the mobile canteen truck of the 28th (Māori) Battalion. The 'gift' was from children in Native Schools who had raised the money by growing and selling vegetables, holding concerts and stalls and emptying their piggy banks. A former commander of the battalion,

The restored 28th Māori Battalion canteen truck at the National Army Museum in Waiouru.

J. C. Henare, told the Duke how the truck had accompanied them through North Africa and Italy in the Second World War. You can still see *Te Rau Aroha*, restored and on display at the National Army Museum in Waiouru.

1970s: An era of change

During the 1970s, Waitangi Day ceremonies were centred chiefly on Northland. New Zealand had been viewed for a long time, both here and overseas, as a country without race relations problems, and the governor-general, Sir Arthur Porritt, could still claim, 'I just do not believe that racism or discrimination exists in this country.' Many people held to this belief, but others were starting to challenge it. And as Māori started to move in large numbers from the country into towns and cities, Duncan MacIntyre (Minister of Māori and Island Affairs) predicted that the new decade would be 'the time for testing our oft-repeated boasts of being one people'.

Māori were trying to get their rights under the Treaty recognised, in an era when many Pākehā still had little interest in or understanding of the Treaty and the issues it raised. Ngā Tamatoa (The Young Warriors) was a protest group that emerged from the Young Māori Leaders Conference at Auckland University in 1970. They campaigned for Māori language and culture to be taught in schools, and they organised the 1975 Māori Land March, led by Whina Cooper, from the Far North to Parliament. On Waitangi Day 1971, they wore wreaths and black

CHANGE, PROTEST AND PROGRESS **33**

Brynderwyn bus tragedy

There was a tragic end to Waitangi Day 1963. A group of Māori men, women and children had travelled north to attend the celebrations and see the Queen. They booked a bus, but because of a last-minute mix-up, it was given to another group and replaced by a much older vehicle. On the return trip on 7 February, on the Brynderwyn hills between Whāngārei and Wellsford, the brakes failed. The driver tried to steer the bus safely to the bottom of the hill, but it failed to take the last bend and went over a bank. Fifteen people died and many others were injured in the worst road crash in New Zealand's history.

The Brynderwyn memorial to the bus victims.

> Asked whether the average Māori cared about Waitangi Day, Mr Kawiti said, 'They have been talking about it for over a hundred years.'
>
> **New Zealand Herald**, 6 February 1971

clothing to symbolise that they wanted to mourn and not celebrate the signing of the Treaty. The following year, Ngā Tamatoa staged a peaceful walkout and called for a total boycott of the celebrations.

Waitangi Day or New Zealand Day?

During its 1957 election campaign, the Labour Party had promised to make 6 February a public holiday. Labour won the election, but the Waitangi Day Act of 1960, which gave 6 February the name of Waitangi Day and called it a 'national day of thanksgiving', didn't make it a public holiday. It became Northland's provincial anniversary day under an Amendment Act passed by the National Government in 1963.

The Third Labour Government, under Prime Minister Norman Kirk, made 6 February a national holiday and renamed it New Zealand Day from 1974. Many people were uncertain about the change of name, and Mr Kirk admitted that in his heart he would still think of it as Waitangi Day. In 1976, the name was changed back again and it has been Waitangi Day ever since. In 2013, the

Baxter, photographed in 1971, soon after he went to protest at Waitangi.

James K. Baxter

Poet James K. Baxter, who had a deep interest in Māori culture and a concern for social injustice, accompanied the protesters on Waitangi Day 1971. When asked about a new mood among the Māori people, he said, 'The pot is on the boil.' Baxter died of a heart attack the following year, aged only 46.

Holidays (Full Recognition of Waitangi Day and ANZAC Day) Amendment Act was passed. This allowed Waitangi Day to be 'Mondayised', so the public holiday can be shifted to a Monday when 6 February falls on a weekend.

WAITANGI DAY

> Sir,—Through the generous gift of Waitangi to the Dominion, Their Excellencies Lord Bledisloe and Lady Bledisloe have undoubtedly made patent to us all the historic value of the Treaty of Waitangi. History tells us that the first signatures to the treaty were made on the morning of Thursday, February 6, 1840, and it seems that that date would be a suitable one to mark as the National Day for New Zealand. A National Day for New Zealand will have to come sooner or later and why not take advantage of the Waitangi celebrations and proclaim it now?   AMY E. MOSS.

This letter to the editor of the *New Zealand Herald*, published 3 February 1934, suggested 6 February as National Day.

Prime Minister Norman Kirk walked with this young Māori boy, Moana Priest, as he moved forward to speak on Waitangi Day 1973.

The 1974 extravaganza

Another royal visit to Waitangi on 6 February 1974 put police on special alert for protests. Small fires were started by Molotov cocktails thrown into bushes, and a bigger one by arsonists who set light to an oil drum. Navy divers rushed to the Waitangi jetty to check reports that a bomb was planted underneath, but it was a false alarm. An explosive device fixed to the Russell flagpole was found during a routine check and failed to go off.

The Queen and her family came ashore from the royal yacht *Britannia* to watch the two-and-a-half-hour 'extravaganza' planned for the first New Zealand Day. The outdoor show, called *Aotearoa*, was broadcast live on television. It depicted the history of New Zealand, beginning with the arrival of Kupe. A moa cavorted around and laid an egg, schoolchildren sang 'Oma Rāpeti', and different cultural groups performed. The finale featured dancers, in flared trousers and kaftans, performing 'The Age of Aquarius' and 'Let the Sunshine In' from the 1970s rock musical *Hair*. Some people thought the show was spectacular, others hated it.

Reactions to the extravaganza

'I thought it was great — real swinging.'

'It was just a stunt — I thought it was never going to end.'

'Good in parts … that Howard Morrison is real funny.'

'It gave me a new idea of history.'

'We made a mockery of some precious things.'

settlement in Australia. Many Pacific nations have a special day to mark when they became self-governing or gained independence.

In his 1974 Waitangi Day speech, Prime Minister Norman Kirk said that some nations celebrated on their national day an act of violence, a revolution or a war, but that New Zealand was different:

We achieved our independence and our nationhood gradually, peacefully. We remember no martyrs who fought to overthrow a tyrant or to drive out an alien power. We were the lucky country. Independence was handed to us on a plate in a friendly, gentlemanly, rational fashion.

National Days

Not every country has a national day, and some have more than one. Australia Day is 26 January, the day in 1788 when the arrival of the First Fleet marked the beginning of British

Royal ascent

6 February is also a special day for Queen Elizabeth II, as it marks the date in 1952 on which she ascended the throne. In 2012, she marked the sixtieth anniversary of her ascension, only the second British monarch to do so.

Queen Elizabeth, Prince Charles, the Duke of Edinburgh, and Norman Kirk attend the New Zealand Day celebrations at Waitangi on 6 February 1974.

Pushing for Treaty recognition

The 1970s was a decade of protests, led by organisations like Friends of the Earth, CARE (Citizens' Association for Racial Equality), and HART (Halt All Racist Tours). Other protests focused on Māori land loss, in particular at Takaparawhā (Bastion Point) in Auckland and the Raglan golf course.

For many years, Māori protests had gone unheard, but now there was growing recognition that their grievances were real. In 1975, the Treaty of Waitangi Act was passed to set up the Waitangi Tribunal. This would act as a permanent commission of inquiry for claims by Māori against the Crown, based on promises made in the Treaty of Waitangi that had since been broken or not kept. (At first these were limited to Crown actions that took place after 1975, but later the Tribunal was given powers to hear claims dating back to 1840.)

The Tribunal met for the first time in 1977, but protesters in Waitangi still shouted 'Honour the Treaty' and 'The Treaty is a fraud'. Ngā Tamatoa handed out pamphlets asking when the Treaty would be given its full recognition so that Māori could stand tall. Media focused on and magnified any protest incidents, with front-page headlines like 'Waitangi marae in uproar' and 'Police swoop on Waitangi protesters'.

Not all Māori supported these protests. Elders on the marae and the young **activists** held different views of the Treaty. The elders felt that the protesters should have the right to put their views across, but they pleaded with them to come in peace, to show respect to the elders, and not to do anything foolish.

In 1981, Graham Latimer and Whina Cooper received their royal honours at Waitangi, but protesters from the Waitangi Action Committee argued that it was wrong to receive 'the Crown's medal' on the marae. (The Waitangi Action Committee was a group that represented both Māori and Pākehā protesters.) When they began to disrupt the **investitures**, police moved in and carted them away to waiting vans. Māori wardens formed a ring to protect Sir Graham; some of the older Māori women broke down and wept. Ben Couch, the Minister of Māori Affairs and Minister of Police (and former All Black and Māori All Black), called for three cheers for Sir Graham Latimer and Dame Whina Cooper. A voice from the crowd replied, 'Three cheers for the young Māoris arrested in defence of their land.'

In between this and the next Waitangi Day came the 1981 Springboks rugby tour, when for the first time ordinary New Zealanders found themselves face to face with police in riot gear. Over the following years, protesters and police faced each other again at Waitangi. In 1982, police went on board the nuclear protest yacht *Pacific Peacemaker* when campaigners from the boat broadcast speeches over a loudspeaker. Governor-General Sir David Beattie was hit by a golf ball and an egg, despite a close police guard. In 1983, police searched people's bags and took sniffer dogs around the grounds, checking for bombs. Squads of police in riot gear and carrying batons stopped and arrested groups of protesters as they made their way across the Waitangi River bridge.

The Church and the Treaty: Christians under arrest

Many people were starting to ask questions about the Treaty and about how Waitangi Day was marked. Some felt that it was wrong to celebrate Waitangi Day. The National Council of Churches of New Zealand (NCC) asked its member churches not to join in any 'celebrations'. In 1983, they issued a Service of Repentance and Hope to be used in churches on Waitangi Day (which was a Sunday).

Nine NCC members travelled to Waitangi, hoping to deliver their message of repentance and the need for education and reconciliation in a direct but non-violent way. Some of them tried to present their own Bible readings and prayers; two men ripped off their shirts to reveal symbolic sackcloth clothing and scattered ashes over their heads. They were all taken away by police and later fined on a charge of disorderly behaviour. Not everyone supported their actions. People both within and outside the churches criticised what they had done.

1984 Hīkoi ki Waitangi

A 250 km **hīkoi** (peace march) from Ngāruawāhia to Waitangi was joined by Māori from different tribes, as well as church leaders and Pākehā. The hīkoi camped at Bastion Point on its way through Auckland. Police guarded the Harbour Bridge in case the marchers tried to cross it on foot, but they piled into buses, vans and cars at Ōrākei Domain and drove over.

> *By your actions, you have sharpened the focus of everyone in New Zealand on the Treaty of Waitangi and on the issue of justice in Māori/Pākehā relations in this country.*
> **Message from the Federation of Labour to the hīkoi**

On Waitangi Day, they gathered at Paihia with others who had arrived by train (dubbed the 'Tainui Express'), and waited at the Waitangi bridge while Governor-General Sir David Beattie went to the Treaty House grounds to meet a deputation. The peace marchers decided that, for the

Hīkoi halted at the bridge at Waitangi, photo by Gil Hanly. On the left, over the Māori warden's hat, Titewhai Harawira can be seen standing near Sue Nikora, Eva Rickard, and Bishop Whakahuihui Vercoe in the front row, with Archbishop Paul Reeves to the right.

sake of unity, they should all meet him. Sir David asked if that would be possible, but police advised against it, and he returned to the Waitangi Hotel without meeting the hīkoi.

Waitangi or Wellington?

The situation at Waitangi seemed to have reached an impasse, with each Waitangi Day marked by conflict and protests, and the Labour Government, under Prime Minister David Lange, shifted the official celebrations to Wellington. The new venue didn't help the 1986 Waitangi Day ceremony; speeches inside the Beehive were barely audible over the noise of protesters chanting, blowing whistles and thumping on car bonnets outside.

Meanwhile, a smaller service at Waitangi went ahead peacefully in brilliant sunshine, but many Māori were disappointed at the lack of any official ceremony. Some had refused the offer of a trip to Wellington because they had been attending the ceremony at Waitangi for so long. A 78-year-old Māori woman who had helped to make the tukutuku panels in the meeting house said, 'We are not one people with some here and some in Wellington.' Dame Whina Cooper brandished her stick and addressed the absent governor-general and prime minister: 'Where are you? This is where you should be and you are not here. It hurts me that you are not here. This is where the Treaty was signed and this is where everyone should be.'

Sir Paul Reeves, the country's first Māori governor-general, belonged to the Puketapu hapū of the Te Āti Awa iwi from Taranaki. When he went north for Waitangi Day 1987, a busload of people from Taranaki set off at 1.30 a.m. so they could join him. This was his Waitangi Day message to the country, 1989:

> Some people may feel resentful at the number of Māori claims. To them I would say, learn something of the history of this land between 1840 and 1870. To the Māori I would say, learn something of the hopes of those people who from 1840 on were prepared to spend four months on a sailing ship to get here.

This 1990 Waitangi commemorative stamp sheet shows a popular reconstruction of the Treaty signing.

In 1990, the Reserve Bank issued a special $10 note to mark 150 years since the signing of the Treaty.

1990: Sesquicentennial

Before 1990, few people had heard of the word 'sesquicentennial', but suddenly it was everywhere. More restoration work was carried out to make the Treaty House appear as it would have done in 1840. Big celebrations were planned to mark 150 years since the signing of the Treaty, but many people felt it would be an empty anniversary. Hone Harawira said, 'One year off 150 years and what have we got to celebrate? Nothing, absolutely nothing.'

On 6 February 1990, the bay was full of boats: navy frigates, tall ships, America's Cup yachts, and 20 waka taua, including the great war canoe *Ngātokimatawhaorua* with its 80 paddlers. Security was tight with hundreds of police present, and several roadblocks set up for the 50,000 people — and many protesters — expected to attend. It was so hot that firemen hosed people down to keep them cool. People in the crowd fainted, and four were taken to hospital with heat exhaustion.

The Queen and Duke of Edinburgh had been at the Commonwealth Games in Auckland, and they arrived at the Waitangi jetty by barge. Some protesters waded into the water and yelled protest slogans and abuse. As the royal couple were being driven up the Nias Track in an open car, a young Māori woman threw a wet black T-shirt at the Queen, which left her visibly shaken. Other protesters chanted 'Go home' when she was speaking.

BISHOP VERCOE'S SPEECH

When Whakahuihui Vercoe, the Bishop of Aotearoa, stood up to speak, the protesters tried to shout him down. Their heckling turned to cheers and applause when he said that the Treaty was a compact that had not been honoured.

One of the many waka at Waitangi for the 1990 celebrations draws near to protesters gathered at Te Tii marae.

Māoritanga — scenes from Māori life, protests and demonstrations, Waitangi, 1990, photo by Ans Westra.

> Some of us have come here to remember what our tūpuna said on this ground: that the Treaty was a compact between two people. But since the signing of that Treaty 150 years ago, I want to remind our partner that you have marginalised us. You have not honoured the Treaty. We have not honoured each other in the promises that we made on this sacred ground.
>
> Since 1840, the partner that has been marginalised is me — the language of this land is yours, the custom is yours, the media by which we tell the world who we are, are yours. The needs and tastes of one partner is addressed in all our advertisements and it makes me sad when we sing 'give me a taste of Kiwi' with a Red Lion can.

This 1990 Waitangi Day speech by Bishop Vercoe has been called one of the great New Zealand sermons of the twentieth century.

Kaupapa Waka — Project Canoe

The Kaupapa Waka project involved Māori from iwi all over New Zealand, who built and carved **waka** and brought them to join *Ngātoki* at Waitangi. They were in all styles, from the traditionally built Moriori waka *Te Rangimata*, made of raupō weeds and mānuka, to Ngāti Ranginui's fibreglass waka *Takitimu* from Tauranga. The waka arrived on the backs of trucks — the *Mataatua* waka was paddled all the way from Doubtless Bay — and were kept under 24-hour guard on the beach at Waitangi. The waka crews had been in training for months, getting fit and learning how to paddle, and also learning about the wairua or spiritual side of waka, and they continued to train out on the bay. When the hull of *Tamatea Ariki Nui* was cracked, everyone pitched in, working day and night to repair it. On Waitangi Day, the waka formed a floating guard of honour for the barge that carried Queen Elizabeth.

Freedom for the navy

There is a special link between the navy and the local community at Waitangi, going back to Captain Hobson and the ships and officers of the Royal Navy.

In 1990, in recognition of this ongoing relationship, the navy was honoured with the presentation of a charter, which granted it the freedom of Te Tai Tokerau. It gives the navy 'the right and privilege, without further permission being obtained, of marching at all times with drums beating, bands playing, colours flying, bayonets fixed and swords drawn through the lands of Te Tai Tokerau, especially the Treaty Ground'.

The Royal Guard of Honour at the Waitangi Treaty Grounds in 2013.

Stevie and Peewee

Through the 1980s, many Pākehā still had little knowledge of the Treaty. Few had ever read it, or realised that there was a difference between the English and the Māori versions. The New Zealand 1990 Commission ran a public education campaign to change this. They filmed a series of TV advertisements which featured two boys, one Māori and one Pākehā. Wayne (or Peewee) Tuapawa lived with his grandmother in Tolaga Bay, and Steve Askin was the son of the Baptist pastor in Ruatoria. The boys were filmed at Anaura Bay as they wandered along the beach, skipped stones on the water and cooked mussels over an open fire on the sand. The bond between them was depicted as a symbol of unity and the Treaty partnership. The 'Stevie and Peewee' advertisements did make a difference. By Waitangi Day 1990, a survey showed that 60 per cent of New Zealanders believed the Treaty was still important, and by the end of the year more than 30 per cent of people said they had read it.

'Stevie' and 'Peewee' from the public education programme of 1990.

The Māori flag

In 1989, a group from the Far North called Te Kawariki held a competition to design a national Māori flag. They came up with the idea after some of them travelled to Australia and saw the Aboriginal flag. Three Māori artists — Hiraina Marsden, Jan Dobson and Linda Munn — designed the winning entry. It was unveiled at Waitangi in 1990 and is now known as the Tino Rangatiratanga flag.

The flag was printed on hats, badges, T-shirts, key rings and stickers, and was used in protests at the Waitangi Treaty Grounds and other places around the country, such as Moutoa Gardens in Whanganui in 1995 and the foreshore and seabed hīkoi in 2004.

Until 2008, Transit New Zealand (now the New Zealand Transport Agency) was in charge of the Auckland Harbour Bridge, and dictated what flags could fly from it. Usually this was the New Zealand flag, but they had flown flags from other countries, and even the yachting Team NZ flag. In 2007, they refused a request from Te Ata Tino Toa, a Māori sovereignty group, to fly the Tino Rangatiratanga flag from the bridge on Waitangi Day. Groups of people climbed One Tree Hill and other Auckland volcanoes to fly the flags from the top of them instead.

In 2009, Māori Party co-leader Pita Sharples called for a national Māori flag to be flown from the bridge on Waitangi Day. The government started a consultation process. Hui took place around the country and over 1200 submissions were received, with 80 per cent in favour of the Tino Rangatiratanga flag. Te Ata Tino Toa sent a thank-you gift to the prime minister, John Key: a T-shirt printed with the flag, addressed to 'Hone Kei, Pirimia'.

On 14 December 2009, Cabinet recognised the Tino Rangatiratanga flag as the preferred national Māori flag, to complement the New Zealand flag. The next year on Waitangi Day it flew on buildings and other sites of national significance, such as Parliament, the National War Memorial, Te Papa Tongarewa and some government departments (and also the Auckland Harbour Bridge). It is not, however, universally supported, and some groups prefer other flags, such as the United Tribes flag.

More protests: 1990s

In the early 1990s, protesters heckled and held up banners but did not disrupt events too much. Prince Charles was mobbed by an enthusiastic crowd in 1994. Mike Smith, a spokesman for Te Kawariki, greeted him with a reminder of some of the first Māori travellers to England:

Your family and mine go back a long way. Our ancestors met and mine said, 'How do you do, king?' Your ancestor replied to my ancestor, 'How do you do, king?' Today, years later, we have the chance to acknowledge each other again.

The Tino Rangatiratanga flag.

The two flags flying at Parliament.

CHANGE, PROTEST AND PROGRESS   41

New Zealand Wars memorial on Marsland Hill

One night in February 1991, the statue of a colonial soldier on Marsland Hill in New Plymouth was smashed to the ground. A sign left behind read: 'In remembrance of the Māori people who suffered in the military campaigns — honour the Treaty of Waitangi.' Today the plinth remains empty; the figure was never replaced.

The memorial on Marsland Hill.

By 1995, there was growing disquiet over the handling of Treaty settlements. Someone tried to set fire to the Treaty House during the night, and an outside wall was scorched before the blaze was put out. The official party was kept waiting before they were welcomed onto the marae. Dame Cath Tizard, the governor-general, was spat on twice. A man trampled on the New Zealand flag. The prime minister, Jim Bolger, had to end his speech when someone unplugged the microphone. Māori elders delivered angry speeches, and protesters yelled, booed and jeered.

In the afternoon, about 600 protesters from Te Kawariki crossed the Waitangi bridge, lowered the official flags and raised their own ones. After a day of conflict and confrontation, it was decided to cancel the evening ceremony. Dame Cath said she was 'deeply grieved' and the cancellation was 'a great loss to tangata whenua who supported the commemoration and who were an integral part of the planning process'.

As a result, the official Waitangi Day ceremonies took place at Government House in Wellington for the next three years, with a smaller service held at Waitangi. But in 1997, the governor-general, Sir Michael Hardie Boys, called for the official ceremony to return to Waitangi, 'the traditional and proper place' to celebrate the signing of the Treaty.

Women on the marae

The events of 1998 were more dramatic and had a lasting impact. They centred around the rights of women to speak on the marae.

Prime Minister Jenny Shipley attended a gathering at the Te Tii marae on 5 February. The Māori kaumātua (elders) were glad to see a representative of the Crown back at Waitangi, and she was given the right to stand and speak during the welcoming ceremony. The next morning, Jenny Shipley returned to Wellington, but Helen Clark, Leader of the Opposition, was present at Te Tii. When she was invited to speak, she was interrupted by Titewhai Harawira, a veteran Māori rights campaigner who had not been there the day before, and who challenged Helen Clark's right, as a

WAITANGI DAY

A mud-splattered Don Brash speaks to the media at Waitangi in 2004.

Prime Minister Helen Clark is escorted off Te Tii Marae in 2004.

Pākehā woman, to speak on the marae, when Māori women could not do so. Helen Clark was deeply upset and reduced to tears by the incident.

The official ceremony returned to Waitangi in 1999, but the underlying tension over this issue remained. In 2000, Clark (by now prime minister) accepted an invitation from Ngāi Tahu to attend a Waitangi Day ceremony at Ōnuku marae. She praised the warm, friendly atmosphere, saying, 'Ngāi Tahu has shown what Waitangi Day can be.' Meanwhile, Titewhai Harawira and a large band of supporters were barred from going onto the marae, and arguments over women's speaking rights continued.

In 2014, women were allowed to speak at Te Tii marae for the first time. One of them, lawyer and politician Annette Sykes, said, 'I think I am part of a continuum of women like Titewhai, like Dame Mira Szászy, who argued for human rights for Māori women to be extended beyond the kitchen, beyond inside the wharenui out on to the marae area.'

The new millennium

In 2004, Prime Minister Helen Clark and Opposition Leader Don Brash faced an even harsher reception than that of 1998. There was widespread anger over the government's policy on foreshore and seabed ownership. Brash was unpopular because of his speech on race relations, delivered to the Orewa Rotary Club a week earlier, and he was pelted with mud at the entrance to the marae. Clark and other MPs were jostled and pushed by protesters. From then on, she chose to go elsewhere on Waitangi Day. Waitangi would always have a special significance, she said, but added that 'all over New Zealand people are reclaiming the day, and they are saying, "We would like to do something with it." There are amazing community events going on from Bluff to the Far North.'

Prime Minister John Key faced several protests at Waitangi, but promised to keep coming to Te Tii, saying it would be hypocritical not to after criticising Helen Clark for staying away. In 2009, when he went to Waitangi with a broken arm, he was shoved and grabbed by two men as he went onto the marae, and couldn't ward them off. The men were later sentenced for assault. In 2013, there was a stand-off between kuia (female elders) as to who would lead him onto Te Tii: Titewhai Harawira or Ani Taurua, a kuia whom the marae had chosen, feeling that she had earned the right after years of washing dishes and preparing food there.

The Year of the Waka

2010 marked the seventieth birthday of *Ngātoki* and was also the Year of the Waka. More than 30 waka — forming the largest fleet in recorded history — gathered at Waitangi for Waitangi Day. Also present was Glass Murray, from Te Kao, the last-known living member of the original crew. Aged 86, he still remembered paddling the waka around hairpin bends from the Kerikeri Inlet to Waitangi, and meeting Te Puea Hērangi of Tainui, who had commissioned it to be built.

Political cartoons of 1997 (top) and 2003 (above) present a different view of Waitangi unrest.

Waka and HMNZS *Te Mana* at Waitangi in 2013.

CHAPTER 4

WAITANGI DAY IN THE 21ST CENTURY

Public attitudes to Waitangi Day

Today the Treaty is recognised as the country's founding document. The spirit of the Treaty and Treaty principles are acknowledged in legislation and referred to in many national organisations.

Waitangi Day itself is still marked by controversy and debate. Some people see it as just another public holiday. For others, it is a time to celebrate family life or their own culture. For a growing number of people all around the country, it is a day to think about the meaning of the Treaty and to enjoy attending Waitangi Day events.

The Beat Retreat and Ceremonial Sunset ceremony. The Governor-General, Sir Jerry Mateparae, reviews the Guard of Honour of the Royal New Zealand Navy.

WAITANGI DAY IN THE 21ST CENTURY   **45**

Waitangi Day celebrations near Ōamaru in 2002.

Waitangi Day is always special for me because I usually go up to Waitangi itself. It is a superb site. So many of our foundations of relationships were laid there — the 1834 flag chosen, the 1835 Declaration of Independence signed, and the 1840 Treaty first presented and signed by some 40 or more chiefs. Each year we recall those events and especially the coming together of two strong cultures to found a new nation. Neither side knew how it would work out and each had different aspirations and plans. We are still working on that relationship — like most relationships it needs caring for. That caring must come through a union of hearts and minds within our nation. Waitangi Day is the time to think on that and to celebrate the steps we are taking every day.

Dame Claudia Orange DNZM OBE, Practice Leader Research, Museum of New Zealand Te Papa Tongarewa

Citizenship ceremony on Waitangi Day, 2012.

What happens at Waitangi

In the days leading up to Waitangi Day, guests and visiting officials are welcomed onto Te Tii marae. Discussions, meetings and workshops are held on the marae on 5 February.

On 6 February, a dawn karakia (prayer service) is held in Te Whare Rūnanga. Other events include the launch of the waka and a 21-gun salute. During the day, there are craft and food stalls, **kapa haka** and a family fun day on the sportsfields. At some stage, there is often a hīkoi from Te Tii to the Treaty Grounds. The navy band performs, and at the end of the day the Beat Retreat ceremony is carried out at the flagpole for the flag lowering.

The Royal New Zealand Navy Māori Culture Group perform at Waitangi in 2010 (above) and the Navy present a 100-man Royal Guard of Honour for the flag lowering ceremony (below).

WAITANGI DAY IN THE 21ST CENTURY 47

What happens around the country

Waitangi Day events include marae open days, community dawn services and picnics, concerts, festivals and family days. Some communities use the day to hold citizenship ceremonies. Governor-General Sir Jerry Mateparae said: 'As Waitangi Day is our national day, I could not think of a better way of recognising the contribution of "new New Zealanders" to our country than to hold a citizenship ceremony to welcome them to our New Zealand family.'

MANGUNGU

In recent years, Waitangi Treaty Day has been held at Mangungu on 12 February. It is a family occasion with picnics, traditional ceremonies and performances, stalls and other entertainment. There have been re-enactments of the signing of the Treaty and, once, a three-day hīkoi taking a group of children from Waimate Mission Station to Mangungu.

KAWHIA KAI FESTIVAL

In Kawhia, Waitangi Day is celebrated with a food festival that includes hāngī, seafood (such as mussels, pāua, kina and īnanga), smoked eel, pūhā and fermented corn.

PORIRUA: FESTIVAL OF THE ELEMENTS

The Festival of the Elements is named for the elements of earth and air, fire and water, which are meaningful in all cultures. It 'uses the arts to celebrate the cultural diversity of Porirua, made possible by the Treaty of Waitangi'.

OKAINS BAY

Waitangi Day has been marked at Okains Bay on Banks

Governor-General Sir Jerry Mateparae's first Waitangi Day address, 6 February 2012:

Waitangi Day represents different things to different people.

It is a day of reflection for some, a time to look back at the tangled roots of our nation's history, recall our achievements, our triumphs and recommit ourselves to reconciling the challenging times of our history.

It is a day of debate for others, when some discuss the significance of the Treaty and its evolving principles in the life of a modern and independent democracy.

It is a day of family time for many.

While Waitangi Day represents different things to different people, it is first and foremost New Zealand's national day.

As our national day, it is a time when we celebrate all that it means to be a New Zealander and take pride in the things that we have achieved in this beautiful land that we call home.

As our national day, it is a time when we reaffirm our commitment to the shared values that bind us together — compassion, tolerance, a strong sense of community and a Kiwi can-do attitude.

And it is a time when we look forward with renewed hope for our country's prospects, confident that the New Zealand we will bequeath to our young people will continue to be a great place to live, to settle and to raise a family.

The Governor-General, Sir Jerry Mateparae, gives his Bledisloe address at Waitangi in 2012.

WAITANGI DAY

Serving traditional Māori food at the Kawhia Kai Fesitval.

Colour and spectacle at the Festival of the Elements in Porirua.

Peninsula since 1977. The celebrations are organised by the local Māori community and the Okains Bay Māori and Colonial Museum.

NGĀI TAHU TREATY FESTIVAL

There were three places in the South Island where Ngāi Tahu signed the Treaty in 1840: Ōnuku, south of Akaroa; Ōtākou, near Dunedin; and Ruapuke Island in Foveaux Strait. The Ngāi Tahu Waitangi Day commemorations circulate around each place in turn. In a three-year cycle, they are held at Ōtākou Marae, Ōnuku Marae, and Rau Aroha Marae at Awarua (Bluff), which lies 20 km north-west of Ruapuke Island. Each year they include important **kōrero** (discussions) about environmental, political and local issues.

Waitangi Day overseas

In London, there is a service at the church of St Lawrence Jewry. On the Saturday closest to Waitangi Day, thousands of Kiwis take part in the Waitangi Day Circle Line Pub Crawl, stopping at pubs on the Circle Line of the Underground and finishing with a haka at Westminster Abbey.

In the USA, Kea New York and the Kiwi Club of New York organise a Waitangi Day event with New Zealand food, wine and beer. In Australia, thousands of people go to the Waitangi Day and Pacific Island Festival at Carrara Stadium on the Gold Coast to celebrate New Zealand and Polynesian music and dancing, and to enjoy traditional hāngī and Polynesian foods, kapa haka performances, carnival rides, market stalls, face-painters and balloon artists.

New Zealand Defence Force (NZDF) personnel overseas organise fun-runs and special meals. 'The ground is frozen solid on most days so digging a hāngī pit in Afghanistan isn't easy,' says Captain Kevin Short. 'We had to wait until a sunny day before we could start digging so the ground was easier to break.'

Ideas for how to celebrate Waitangi Day

- Go along to a Waitangi Day event in your local area.
- Organise a trip to Waitangi itself.
- If you are in Wellington, go and look at the original copies of the Treaty of Waitangi currently on permanent display in the Constitution Room at Archives New Zealand.
- Read the Treaty online, at http://www.nzhistory.net.nz/politics/treaty/read-the-treaty/english-text

WAITANGI DAY IN THE 21ST CENTURY 49

ABOVE AND BELOW: Kiwis in London celebrating Waitangi Day.

- Read a book, look at a website or go to a museum to find out about New Zealand history.
- Follow the news on radio, TV, newspapers or online about what is happening in Waitangi Day across the country.
- Do something fun with your family.
- Talk about your family history or **whakapapa**.
- Hold a neighbourhood barbecue, pot-luck meal or get-together.
- Put down a hāngī or prepare some other New Zealand food.
- Read a book by a Kiwi author, listen to Kiwi music, or watch a Kiwi movie.
- Play some reggae music. (Waitangi Day is also Bob Marley's birthday.)
- Go along to a music festival.
- Keep New Zealand clean and beautiful: pick up litter, clean up a beach, plant trees, do some gardening.
- Go for a walk and enjoy the outdoors.
- Play sport.
- Enjoy a swim in a river or lake or at the beach.
- Listen to an excerpt from Bishop Vercoe's 1990 speech online at http://www.teara.govt.nz/en/video/27682/bishop-vercoe-at-waitangi-1990, or at http://www.radionz.co.nz/collections/treatyofwaitangi/events1990s
- Watch Māori TV coverage.

Defence Force personnel dig a hāngī pit in Afghanistan.

CHAPTER 5

VISITING WAITANGI: WHAT TO SEE

What you see at Waitangi

Entry to the Waitangi National Reserve was free until 1937, when a one-shilling entry fee was charged for adults. Today, entry is free for children up to the age of 18 with a parent or caregiver, and there is an entry fee for overseas visitors, while New Zealand residents are charged a concessionary rate.

1. TREATY HOUSE

Home to British Resident James Busby and his family, and one of New Zealand's most visited historic buildings. On 5 February 1840, Hobson and others came through the front door into the parlour on the right, where they discussed the final wording of the Treaty before leaving through the French doors onto the verandah to meet the crowds gathered outside.

2. TE WHARE RŪNANGA: THE MEETING HOUSE

A traditional carved meeting house, opened on 6 February 1940 as part of the Centennial celebrations. It is a symbol of tribal unity, because its carvings — created under principal carver Pine Taiapa — include regional styles from all over New Zealand and are not identified with any one tribal ancestor. The meeting house and Treaty House stand close together, representing the equal partnership embodied in the Treaty.

The Treaty House today.

VISITING WAITANGI: WHAT TO SEE **51**

Waitangi Treaty Grounds

Waitangi Golf Club

To Mt Bledisloe

2 TE WHARE RŪNANGA

1 TREATY HOUSE

3 THE FLAGSTAFF

4 Nias Track

8 Camellia Walk

6 TE KOROWAI O MAIKUKU

5 Hobson's Beach

7 VISITOR CENTRE

10 KĪ-O-RAHI FIELD

Tau Henare Drive

Waitangi River bridge

Ti Point

9 TE TII MARAE

Te Ti Bay

Te Whare Rūnanga, the meeting house.

3. THE FLAGSTAFF

The flagstaff (flagpole) — put up in 1934, and replaced by the navy in 1947 when the wood started to rot — marks the spot where the Treaty was signed. Three flags fly from it: the Union Jack, the New Zealand flag and the 1834 Flag of the United Tribes of New Zealand. The flagstaff has often been a focus for protest activities, with protesters trying to scale it to raise their own flags.

4. NIAS TRACK

This is the track along which Captain Hobson and Captain Nias walked on 5 and 6 February 1840.

5. HOBSON'S BEACH

The beach where Captain Hobson landed, and from which the waka are launched. Somewhere near here was Te Ana o Maikuku (the cave of Maikuku).

The Waitangi flagstaff.

VISITING WAITANGI: WHAT TO SEE   **53**

Te Korowai o Maikuku, the waka house.

6. TE KOROWAI O MAIKUKU: THE WAKA HOUSE

This contains *Ngātokimatawhaorua*, the world's largest ceremonial war canoe. Also on display is the stump of the kauri tree from which the bow and stern sections were taken.

7. VISITOR CENTRE

Opened in 1983, the visitor centre was designed by John Scott (1924–1992), who grew up in Hawke's Bay as the third of seven children of English, Irish, Māori and Scottish descent. His architectural style combined Māori and Pākehā features. He designed other public buildings such as Futuna Chapel in Wellington, the Māori Battalion Memorial Community Centre in Palmerston North, and the Te Urewera National Park Headquarters (now the Aniwaniwa Visitor Centre).

8. CAMELLIA WALK

The Treaty Grounds include bush walks and notable trees, including the oldest camellias in New Zealand, planted by James or Agnes Busby in 1833. The large Norfolk pine on the lawn grew from a seedling brought over from Norfolk Island in 1836.

Interior of Te Whare Rūnanga, the meeting house.

ABOVE AND LEFT: Te Tii marae and the memorial that carries text from Te Tiriti o Waitangi.

9. TE TII MARAE

The marae includes the meeting hall (marae ātea), dining hall (whare kai), and other buildings. At dawn on 4 February 1990, the Reverend Māori Marsden held a dedication ceremony of the tau rangatira (guardians), which were carved from old poles from the Opua wharf to mark the spot at the eastern end of the marae where rangatira debated the Treaty on 5 February 1840.

10. KĪ-O-RAHI FIELD: TE ATA-RAU-A-RANGI-HAE-ATA

This field near the Treaty Grounds is dedicated to the ball game kī-o-rahi, which is played with a kī (flax ball), central target (tupu) and seven carved boundary posts (poupou). The game is still known in Italy and France, after the Māori Battalion introduced it there in the Second World War.

Blessing the Kī-o-rahi poupou decorated by students from Opua Primary School.

Places to visit around Waitangi

11. HOHI BAY AND MARSDEN CROSS
Hohi Bay is also known as Oihi Bay. The Oihi Mission Station was the first permanent European settlement in New Zealand. Marsden Cross marks the spot where Samuel Marsden preached his Christmas Day sermon in 1814.

12. STONE STORE AND KEMP HOUSE
The Stone Store and Kemp House both date back to the Kerikeri Mission Station. On display at Kemp House is the writing slate used at the mission school by Rongo, daughter of Ngāpuhi leader Hongi Hika and later wife of Hone Heke. An upstairs room in the Stone Store was home to Bishop Selwyn's library; his wife Sarah said, 'It is by far the nicest room in New Zealand.'

13. KORORIPŌ HISTORIC RESERVE
Kororipō pā was a Ngāpuhi fishing village that was used by Hongi Hika in the 1820s. The track from the Stone Store follows the path made by the missionaries between the pā and the new mission station.

Department of Conservation archaeological dig at Hohi Bay, 2013. Professor Ian Smith, in charge of the operation, said, 'It is difficult to think of a site in New Zealand that is of more importance than this.'

14. WAIMATE NORTH
Te Waimate Mission House was built in 1832. The settlement included a farm, church, school, water mill, blacksmith and brickyard, as well as stables and carpenter shops. Charles Darwin visited here, and it was the second place where the Treaty of Waitangi was signed.

15. MT BLEDISLOE
The viewpoint overlooks Waitangi and the Bay of Islands. It is named after Lord Bledisloe, who also donated the ceramic marker, showing the distances to local sites and overseas cities.

The Stone Store and Kemp House at Kerikeri.

16. PAIHIA
St Paul's Church has a stained-glass window to mark the Williams family's 175-year reunion in 1998. The cemetery contains historic graves, as well as a plaque that records how Māori and Europeans gathered to meet James Busby in May 1833, and to witness the Great Seal on the royal letter being broken so that his appointment as British Resident could be read out. From Paihia the passenger ferry crosses to Russell.

17. OPUA
Opua has a large marina and is a port of entry for yachts from overseas. The car ferry crosses from here to Okiato.

18. OKIATO HISTORIC RESERVE
The government buildings burnt down in 1842, and nothing is left of Hobson's first capital except for the remains of a well.

19. AUCKS ROAD
During the Second World War, the 2nd Battalion of the 3rd Auckland Regiment (nicknamed the Aucks) was based at Russell Camp. The soldiers built the road from Okiato to Russell, known as Aucks Road.

Te Waimate Mission House.

The ceramic marker on Mt Bledisloe.

VISITING WAITANGI: WHAT TO SEE 57

The Pompallier Mission and Printery, Russell.

Mummified rat, Pompallier House. Rats feasted on animal by-products left over from the tanning process and lived in the thick earthen walls, which preserved them when they died. The collection includes mummified rats lying amongst the shreds of leather, paper and clothing they used to line their nests.

20. POMPALLIER MISSION, RUSSELL

The Pompallier Mission is New Zealand's oldest Catholic building and oldest industrial building. Guided tours show how it was built (in a French style called *pisé de terre*), how the tannery turned animal skins into leather, and how thousands of books were hand-printed and bound.

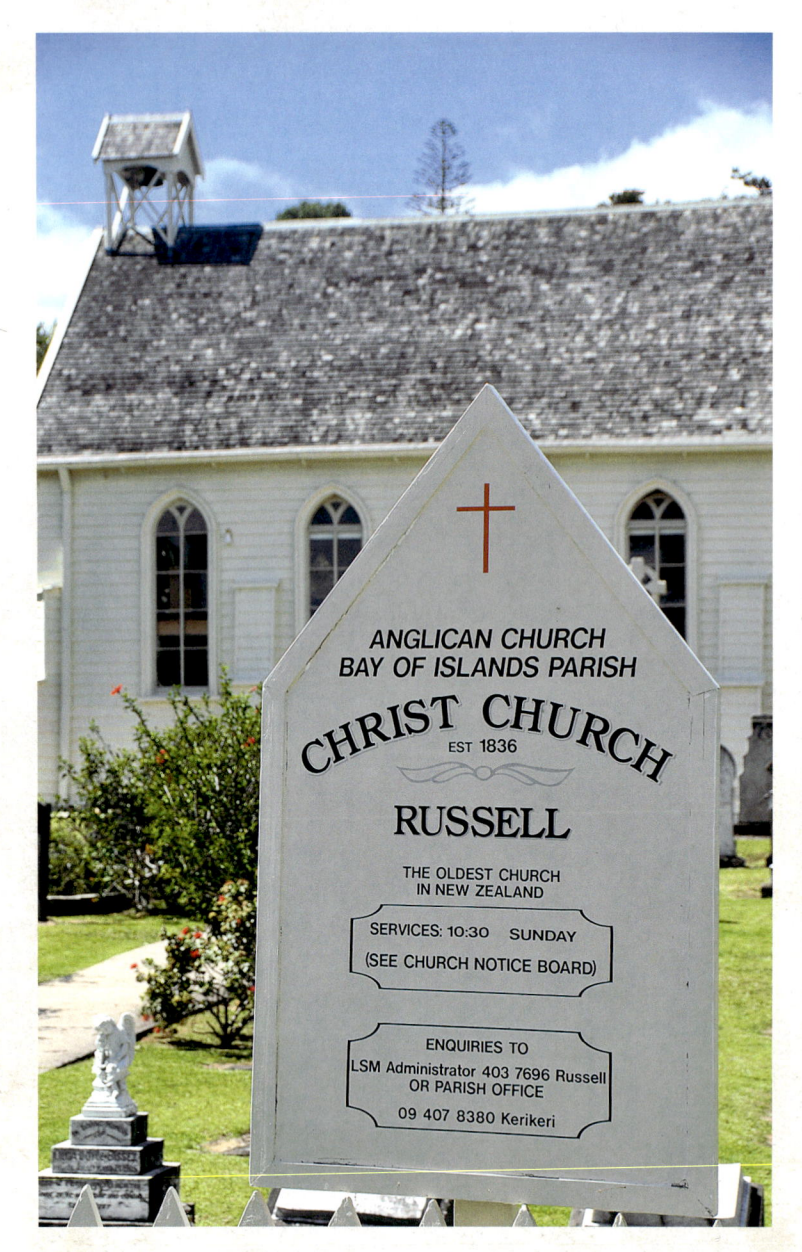

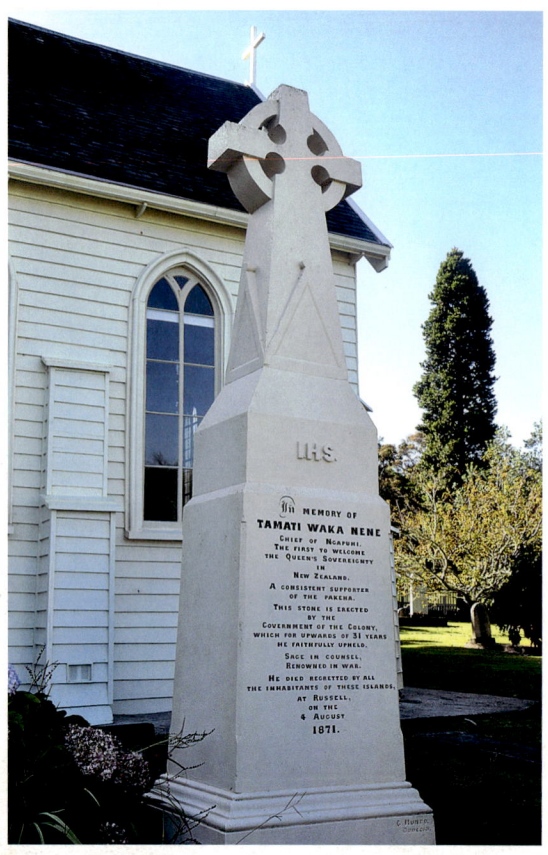

ABOVE: Grave of Tamati Waka Nene, who spoke and fought in favour of the Treaty.

LEFT: Christ Church at Russell is the oldest chuch in New Zealand.

21. FLAGSTAFF HILL HISTORIC RESERVE (MAIKI HILL)

This is where the flagstaff was cut down four times in 1844–45. It was re-erected in 1858, then burnt down in a gorse fire in 1913, repaired and shortened, and put up once more. Lightning shattered the top of it in 1978, but this sixth one still stands today. From here, you can look directly across to the Waitangi flagstaff.

22. CHRIST CHURCH

The oldest surviving church in New Zealand. Holes in the wooden walls were made by musket balls that were fired in the 1845 Battle of Kororāreka.

23. RUSSELL MUSEUM

The collection contains moa bones, whaling equipment, old logbooks and cannon balls.

24. WAITATA POINT HISTORIC RESERVE

You can walk out to Waitata Point at low tide from Long Beach in Russell to see the remains of the coastal battery that operated from September 1943 to November 1944.

25. MT TIKITIKIOURE

Manganese, used in glass and steel making, was mined here through the 1870s and 80s. Buckets of ore travelled 2 km on an overhead wire tramway to ships moored in the bay. The empty buckets were filled with coal, timber and stores for the return trip up to the mining camp.

26. KAWAKAWA

The colourful and quirky public toilets at Kawakawa were designed by Austrian artist Friedensreich Hundertwasser. The Bay of Islands Vintage Railway runs down the middle of the main street.

27. MANGUNGU

The third Treaty signing was at a Wesleyan mission station at Mangungu, near Horeke on the Hokianga harbour. Thousands of Māori arrived in canoes on 12 February 1840, and more rangatira signed the Treaty here than anywhere else in the country. The restored house (which has been to Onehunga and back) contains the table where the Treaty was signed.

WALKS

The walks in this area include parts of Te Araroa (a 3000 km walking track from Cape Reinga to Bluff). The Full Circle Day Walk takes you from Paihia to Opua and Russell and back to Paihia, using the car ferry and passenger ferry. The 6 km Waitangi to Haruru Falls walk goes through mangrove forest and alongside the Waitangi River. Much of this area is a Kiwi Zone where no dogs are allowed. You can also walk the 16 km Cape Brett Track to the Cape Brett Lighthouse, first lit in 1910. The original lighthouse keeper's house can be booked with DOC for overnight stays.

Wesleyan Mission at Mangungu.

THE ISLANDS

- Moturua Island — where du Fresne stayed in 1722 (page 8)
- Motuarohia (or Roberton Island) — where Cook anchored (page 8).

Project Island Song is a campaign to restore ecological balance to these islands and reintroduce native animal and bird species.

Car ferry travelling between Opua and Okiato.

Glossary

activist someone who believes strongly in a cause and takes protest action as a result
anthropologist a scientist who studies how people behave
colony an area or country that is controlled by another country, often far away
confederation an alliance or group of people who agree to work together
covenant a formal promise or agreement
Crown the ruling monarch (either king or queen), or the government of the country under a monarch
gospel the life and teachings of Jesus Christ
grievance an issue or ruling felt to be wrong or unfair
hīkoi a peaceful protest in the form of a walk or march, often over a long distance
hui meeting or gathering
in perpetuity forever
investiture the ceremony for presenting a special title or award
kapa haka Māori cultural or performing group or performance
kōrero talk or speech
man o' war a warship armed with guns and cannons; named after 'men of war', or armed soldiers
native the term often used for 'Māori' in the nineteenth century (and later)
naturalist a scientist who studies natural history, especially plants and animals
pōwhiri formal welcome onto a marae
prefabricated built in parts or sections that can be put together later
Resident a diplomatic representative who exercises some form of indirect rule
tannery a place where animal skins and hides are turned into leather
taua muru a plundering expedition or war party
waka canoe
waka taua the biggest waka, used by war parties
whakapapa genealogy
whare rūnanga meeting house

Timeline

1000 YEARS AGO (APPROX.) Kupe and Ngake (or Ngahue) are the first Polynesian navigators to reach the Bay of Islands.
NOV–DEC 1769 Captain Cook and Joseph Banks arrive in the *Endeavour*.
MAY–JULY 1772 French expedition led by Marc Joseph Marion du Fresne.
25 DEC 1814 Reverend Samuel Marsden delivers Christmas Day sermon at Rangihoua.
17 MAY 1833 James Busby arrives at Paihia on the *Imogene* as first British Resident.
1834 Choosing a national flag.
28 OCT 1835 Declaration of Independence signed.
DEC 1835 Charles Darwin visits in the *Beagle*.
29 JAN 1840 Captain William Hobson arrives on the *Herald* with a rough draft of the Treaty.
5 FEB 1840 Hui at Waitangi.
6 FEB 1840 Signing of the Treaty (Te Tiriti) at Waitangi.
1840 Copies of the Treaty (Te Tiriti) taken around the country for further signings.
FEB 1841 Capital transferred to Auckland.
JUL 1844–MAR 1845 Hone Heke chops down the flagstaff four times.
11 MAR 1845 Battle of Kororāreka.
23 MAR 1881 Opening of the meeting house at Te Tii.
JAN–FEB 1890 Fiftieth anniversary of the founding of New Zealand.
MAY 1932 Lord and Lady Bledisloe buy the Treaty House and grounds.
FEB 1934 The Bledisloes' gift is handed over to the nation at Waitangi.
6 FEB 1940 Centenary of the signing of the Treaty.
28 DEC 1953 Royal visit by Queen Elizabeth II and Prince Philip.
1960 Waitangi Day Act 1960: 6 February to be called Waitangi Day.
1973 Waitangi Day renamed New Zealand Day and made a public holiday.
1976 Name changed back to Waitangi Day.
1975 Treaty of Waitangi Act passed to establish the Waitangi Tribunal.
6 FEB 1990 Sesquicentennial (150 years) celebrations.

Further reading

Websites

Archives NZ: http://archives.govt.nz/exhibitions/treaty

Christchurch City Libraries: http:/christchurchcitylibraries.com/society/culture/holidays/waitangiday/

Heritage New Zealand: Treaty House: http://www.heritage.org.nz/the-list/details/6

Ministry for Culture and Heritage: http://www.mch.govt.nz/nz-identity-heritage/treaty-waitangi

NZ Film Archive: http://www.filmarchive.org.nz/
Films that can be searched for include original newsreels from 1934, *Historic Bay of Islands, a school journey* (1946), *Waitangi Day 1990* (a re-enactment of the signing of the Treaty), the 1990 Stevie and Peewee advertisements, (http://www.ngataonga.org.nz/sellebration/view.php?id=182), *Waitangi: what really happened* (a dramatisation of the events of February 1840), and the Māori TV documentary *The Navy and the Treaty* (2008).

NZ History online: http://www.nzhistory.net.nz/politics/treaty/waitangi-day

The Treaty House: http://www.nzhistory.net.nz/politics/treaty/waitangi-day/the-treaty-house

Treaty FAQs and printable booklets: http://www.nzhistory.net.nz/politics/treaty/treaty-faqs#WherecanIobtainprintedbookletsabouttheTreaty

NZ OnScreen: *Documentary of New Zealand Day at Waitangi 1974*, http://www.nzonscreen.com/title/new-zealand-day-at-waitangi-1974

Te Karere: Waitangi Day 1984 (the Tainui Express and the 1984 hīkoi)
http://www.nzonscreen.com/title/te-karere-1984

Radio NZ: Waitangi Day broadcasts, http://www.radionz.co.nz/national/programmes/waitangiday/20140206

Sound archive of Treaty of Waitangi events, http://www.radionz.co.nz/collections/treatyofwaitangi

Russell Museum: http://www.russellmuseum.org.nz/index.html

Te Ara: Public holidays : http://www.teara.govt.nz/en/public-holidays/page-5

Waitangi Day protests: http://www.teara.govt.nz/en/nga-ropu-tautohetohe-Maori-protest-movements/page-2

Te Papa Tongarewa: Glass Treaty, http://www.tepapa.govt.nz/Education/OnlineResources/SGR/Pages/GlassTreaty.aspx

Signs of a nation: http://tpo.tepapa.govt.nz/ViewExhibitionDetail.asp?Language=English&ExhibitionID=0x000a428f

Treaty2u (exhibition): http://www.treaty2u.govt.nz/

Interactive CD Rom: http://www.treaty2u.govt.nz/cool-stuff/cd-rom/index.htm

Waitangi: http://www.paihia.co.nz/Waitangi.cfm

Waitangi Treaty Grounds: http://www.waitangi.org.nz/index.htm

Waitangi Tribunal: http://www.justice.govt.nz/tribunals/waitangi-tribunal

Books

CHILDREN'S NON-FICTION

Calman, Ross, *The Treaty of Waitangi*, Reed, Auckland, 2003.

CHILDREN'S FICTION

Beale, Fleur, *Mission Girl: The writings of Atapo, Paihia, c1840*, Scholastic, Auckland, 2010. (Originally published as *A New Song in the Land*, 2004.)

De Roo, Anne, *Jacky Nobody*, Methuen, Auckland, 1983.

Menefy, Diana, *Shadow of the Boyd*, HarperCollins, Auckland, 2010.

Morris, Paula, *Hene and the Burning Harbour*, Puffin, Auckland, 2013.

GENERAL HISTORY

Ell, Sarah, *'There she blows': Sealing and whaling days in New Zealand*, Bush Press, Auckland, 1995.

Harris, Aroha, *Hīkoi: Forty years of Māori protest*, Huia Publishers, Wellington, 2004.

King, Michael, *The Penguin History of New Zealand*, Penguin, Auckland, 2003.

O'Malley, Vincent, *The Meeting Place: Māori and Pākehā encounters, 1642–1840*, Auckland University Press, 2012.

Walker, Ranginui, *Ka Whawhai Tonu Matou: Struggle Without End*, Penguin, Auckland, 2004.

THE TREATY OF WAITANGI

Abel, Sue, *Shaping the News: Waitangi Day on television*, Auckland University Press, Auckland, 1997.

Colenso, William, *The Authentic and Genuine History of the Signing of the Treaty of Waitangi*, Government Printer, Wellington, 1890.

Orange, Claudia, *An Illustrated History of the Treaty of Waitangi*, Bridget Williams Books, Wellington, 2004.

——, *The Treaty of Waitangi*, Bridget Williams Books, Wellington, 2011.

——, *The Story of a Treaty*, Bridget Williams Books, Wellington, 2013.

Stenson, Marcia, *The Treaty: Every New Zealander's guide to the Treaty of Waitangi*, Random House, Auckland, 2004.

THE BAY OF ISLANDS

Buick, T. Lindsay, *Waitangi Ninety-four Years After*, Thomas Avery & Sons, New Plymouth, 1934.

Gavalas, Marios, *Landmarks of the Bay of Islands: Past and present*, Raupo, Auckland, 2008.

Lee, Jack, *The Bay of Islands*, Reed, Auckland, 1996.

McLean, Martin, 'The garden of New Zealand: A history of the Waitangi Treaty House and Grounds from pre-European times to the present', Department of Conservation Science and Research Internal Report No. 76, Wellington, 1990.

Ramsden, Eric, *Busby of Waitangi: H.M.'s Resident at New Zealand, 1833–40*, A. H. & A. W. Reed, Auckland, 1942.

Picture credits

Alexander Turnbull Library, Wellington, New Zealand: cover; p.4, cover; p.8; p.9; p.10 (top); p.11 (right); p.12 (top); p.13; p.14 (bottom); cover, p.17 (top); (bottom); p.18; p.20 (top); p.21 (top); cover, (bottom); p.22 (bottom); cover, p.23 (top); (bottom); p.24 (bottom); p.25 (top); (middle); cover, p.26 (top) © Leonard Mitchell; p.31; p.33 (bottom); p.34 (top left); p.35; cover, p.39 (bottom); p.43 (top) © Bob Brockie; (middle) © Allan Hawkey

Archives New Zealand Te Rua Mahara o te Kāwanatanga: p.3, p.29; p.14 (top)

Auckland Libraries, Sir George Grey Special Collections: p.25 (bottom); p.28 (top and bottom)

Daisy Day: p.48 (top left)

Department of Conservation/Te Papa Atawhai: p.55 (bottom)

Destination Northland: p.10 (bottom)

Fairfax NZ: p.42 (top left); (top right)

Government House: p.44; p.45 (bottom); p.47

Gil Hanly: p.36

Heritage New Zealand Pouhere Taonga: p.56 (top); p.57 (middle); p.59

Kiwi Greens UK/Bryce Groves: p.49 (top); (middle)

Macmillan Brown Library: cover, p.16 (top)

Manatū Taonga/Ministry for Culture and Heritage: p.33 (top) © Tim Shoebridge; p.41 © David Green

Geoff Marshall, courtesy of Festival of the Elements 2014: p.48 (top right)

National Museum of the Royal New Zealand Navy: p.30 (bottom)

New Zealand Defence Force: p.32; p.49 (bottom)

The New Zealand Herald: p.34 (top right)

New Zealand Post: cover, p.26 (bottom); p.37 (top)

The Northern Advocate: p.27 (bottom) © Michael Cunningham; p.38 (top)

Reserve Bank of New Zealand: cover, p.27 (top left); p.37 (bottom)

Royal New Zealand Navy: p.39 (top); p.43 (bottom); p.46 (top); (bottom)

Russell Museum/Te Whare Taonga Kororāreka: p.15 (bottom); p.24 (top); p.27 (top right); p.30 (top)

Shutterstock: cover

University Museum of Zoology, Cambridge: p.15 (top)

Waitangi National Trust: p.6; p.20 (bottom); p.52; p.54 (top)

David Werry: p.11 (left); p.12 (bottom); p.19; p.22 (top); p.40 (bottom); p.50; p.52 (bottom); p.53 (top); (bottom); p.54 (top left); (top right); p.56 (middle); (bottom); p. 57 (top); p.58 (top left); (top right); p.59 (bottom)

Ans Westra: p.38 (bottom)

Nanette Wright: p.45 (top)

Index

Page numbers in **bold** refer to illustrations.

Askin, Steve 39, **39**
Aucks Road 56

Baxter, James K. 33, **33**
Bay of Islands (Te Pēwhairangi) **7**, 7–8, 15, 18, 29, **30, 55,** 55–59, *see also* names of individual places, for example Kerikeri
Bledisloe, Lord and Lady 21, **21,** 22, 24, 55
Brash, Don 42, **42**
Brynderwyn bus tragedy 33, **33**
Busby, Agnes 12, 20–21, 53
Busby family gravestone, Paihia **12**
Busby, James 12, **12,** 13, 15, 18, 20, 26, 27, 50, 53, 56
Busby, Sarah (later Sarah Williams) 12, 13

Camellia Walk, Waitangi **51,** 53
centennial of New Zealand (1940) 24, **24, 26,** 26–27, **27,** 28, 29
Christ Church, Russell 15, 58
Clark, Helen 41–42, **42**
Cook, James 8
Cooper, Dame Whina 17, 32, 35, 37
Crozet, Julien 8

Darwin, Charles 10, 15, 55
Declaration of Independence (He Wakaputanga o te Rangatiratanga o Nu Tīreni) 14, **14,** 45

Earle, Augustus 10, **10**
Elizabeth II, Queen and Philip, Duke of Edinburgh 31–32, 33, 34, **35,** 38, 39

fiftieth anniversary of New Zealand (1890) 20
flags of New Zealand 13, **13,** 18, 24, **30,** 40, **40,** 41, 45, 52
Flagstaff Hill Historic Reserve (Maiki Hill) 18, 58
flagstaff, Waitangi 30, 52

French settlement of New Zealand 14–15

Hall, William, and family 9–10, 12
Harawira, Hone 38
Harawira, Titewhai **36,** 41–42, 43
'He iwi tahi tātou' 16, 26
Heke Pokai (Hone Heke) 16, 18, **18,** 26
hīkoi ki Waitangi 36, **36**
Hobson, William 14–15, **15,** 16, **16,** 18, 20, 26, 27, 50
Hobson's Beach **15,** 51, 52
Hohi (Oihi) Bay 9, **11,** 55, **55**
Hokianga 10, 12, 13, 14
Hongi Hika 9, 10, **10,** 11, 18, 55
hui 15–16, 20, 22–23, **23**

Kaupapa Waka project 39
Kawakawa 59
Kawhia Kai Festival 47
Kemp House, Kerikeri 55, **56**
Kendall, Thomas 9–10, 11
Kerikeri 10, 11, 55, **56**
Key, John 40, 43
Kingitanga (Māori King movement) 19, 24, 27, 31
Kingsford-Smith, Sir Charles 25
kī-o-rahi field (Te Ata-Rau-a-Rangi-Hae-Ata) 54, **54**
Kirk, Norman 33, 34, **34**
Korokī (fifth Māori King) 24, 27
Kororāreka (now Russell) 9, 10, 12, **14,** 15, 18, **18,** 34, **57,** 57–58
Kororipō pā/Historic Reserve 12, 55
Kotahitanga mo te Tiriti o Waitangi (Māori Parliament) 19
Kupe 7, 27, 34

Maikuku 8, 52
Mangungu 18, 47, 59, **59**
Māori Battalion 28, **28,** 32, **32,** 54
Māori flags 13, 18, 40, **40,** 41, 45, 52
Māori land loss 15, 19, 32, 35
Māori Land March (1975) 32
Māori Treaty rights, claims and settlements 32–33, 35–37, 41
Māori world view (Te ao Māori) 11

Marion du Fresne, Marc Joseph 8
Markham, Edward 9
Marsden Cross **11,** 55
Marsden, Samuel 9, 11, 55
Marsland Hill New Zealand Wars memorial 41, **41**
Mateparae, Sir Jerry **44,** 47, **47**
missionaries 9–13, 15, 16, 18, 55
Motuarohia (or Roberton) Island 8, 59
Moturua Island 8, 59
Mt Bledisloe 22, **22,** 55, **56**
Mt Tikitikioure 58–59

National Council of Churches of New Zealand 36
national days 34
Native Land Court 19
navy 30, 39, **44, 46,** 52
New Zealand Day 26, 33, 34
New Zealand Wars 18, 19, 20, 41, **41**
Ngā Tamatoa (The Young Warriors) 32–33, 35
Ngāi Tahu Treaty Festival 48
Ngake (Ngāhue) 7
Ngāpuhi 7–8, 9, 11, 12, 16, 18, 20, 27, 55
Ngata, Sir Āpirana 20, 23, 24, **24**
Ngātokimatawhaorua (waka taua) 26, **26–27,** 27, 38, 39, 43, **43,** 53, **53**
Nias, Captain 15, 16, 26, 52
Nias Track 26, 38, **51,** 52
Northern War 18, 20, 58

Okains Bay 47–48
Okiato 18, 56
Opua 22, 23, 28, 54, 56

Paihia 9, 10, 11, 56
Pompallier, Jean-Baptiste 12
Pompallier Mission, Russell 29, 57, **57**
Porirua Festival of the Elements 47, **48**
Priest, Moana 34
protests 32–33, 34, 35–37, **38,** 40, 41–43, 52

Rangihoua pā 9, 10, 11
Reeves, Sir Paul **36,** 37

Rongo, Hariata (Harriet) 18, 55
royal visits 31–32, 33, 34, **35**, 38, 39, 40
Russell (earlier name was Kororāreka) 9, 10, 12, **14**, 15, 18, **18**, 34, **57**, 57–58
Russell Museum 58

school camps 30
sealers 8
Second World War 26, 28, 29, 30, 54, 56
sesquicentennial of New Zealand (1990) **37**, 38
Stone Store, Kerikeri 55, **56**

taua muru 10
Taurua, Ani 43
Te Ana o Maikuku (the cave of Maikuku) 8, 52
Te Korowai o Maikuku (the Waka House) **51**, 53, **53**
Te Puea Herangi 17, 27, 43
Te Rau Aroha (mobile canteen truck of Māori Battalion) 32, **32**
Te Rau-o-te-Rangi, Kahe 17

Te Tii marae 12, **19**, 19–20, **20, 22, 23**, 32, 41–43, **42**, 45, 54, **54**
Te Tiriti o Waitangi meeting house (Waitangi Treaty Hall) **19**, 19–20, **20**
Te Waimate Mission House 55, **56**
Te Whare Rūnanga (The Meeting House) 24, 27, 50, **52, 53**
Topeora, Rangi 17, **17**
traders 9, 18
Treaty House, Waitangi 20–21, **21, 22, 23**, 26, 32, 38, 50, **50**
Treaty of Waitangi 6–7, 12, 15–18, **16–17**, 19, 44–45, 55, 59
    anniversary celebrations **15**, 20, 26–27, **27**, 28, 29, 30, 32–34, **37** (*see also* Waitangi Day)
    Māori language version, Te Tiriti o Waitangi 15, 18, 20
    original documents 29, **29**
Tuapawa, Wayne (Peewee) 39, **39**

Union Jack 13, 18, 24, **30**, 52
Vercoe, Whakahuihui **36**, 38
Visitor Centre, Waitangi **51**, 53

Waikato (Māori chief) 9, 11
Waimate North 11, 15, 18, 55, **56**
Waitangi 8, 9–11, 12, 20–21, 50–54
Waitangi celebrations of Bledisloes' gift (1934) 22–23, **23, 24, 25**
Waitangi Day 6, 32–34, 35–36, 37, 38, 40, 41–43, 44–48, **44–49**
    ideas for how to celebrate 48–49
Waitangi National Reserve **6**, 21–22, 50, **51**
Waitangi National Trust Board 22, **22**
Waitangi Treaty memorial 20, **20**
Waitangi Tribunal 35, 41
Waitata Point Historic Reserve 58
waka taua (war canoes) **8**, 26, **26–27**, 27, 38, 39, 43, **43**, 53, **53**
whalers 8, 9, **9**
Williams, Henry 8, 12, 13, 15, 16, 17
women, Māori 17, 20, 41–42
women, speaking rights on marae 41–42

Acknowledgements

Many people have generously given of their time and expertise to help me in writing this book. In particular, I would like to thank Claudia Orange and David Green (Editor/Historian, Manatū Taonga — Ministry for Culture and Heritage) who agreed to look over an earlier draft of the text for me. I would also like to thank the many wonderful librarians, archivists and historians who have helped, including those at Wellington Public Library, the Alexander Turnbull Library (especially Kim McClintock), Archives NZ, Auckland City Libraries and the Macmillan Brown Library, University of Canterbury. Thanks also to Greg McManus, Nineke Metz and Kate Martin (Waitangi National Trust), Dolores Ho (National Army Museum), Shelley Arlidge (Russell Museum), Paul Stein (NZ Defence Force), Alan Hollows (NZ Post), Neill Atkinson, Steve Watters, Jamie Mackay and Melanie Lovell-Smith (Ministry for Culture and Heritage), Jo Blick (Government House), Raewyn Peters (Reserve Bank), Lesley Brice and Natalie McCondach (Heritage New Zealand Pouhere Taonga), Judit Farquhar-Nadasi (Department of Conservation), Ann Martin-Stacy and Michael Wynd (Torpedo Bay Navy Museum), James Taylor (NZ Film Archive), Bryce Groves (London branch co-convener, Green Party of Aotearoa NZ), Polly Hodgson (University Museum of Zoology, Cambridge), Anne Te Maiharoa-Dodds (Waitaha Taiwhenua o Waitaki Trust Board Inc), Nanette Wright, Bruce Gatward-Cook, Daisy Day, Allan Hawkey and Bob Brockie, Gil Hanly and Ans Westra.

New Holland Publishers have been, as always, amazing to work with. Thanks especially to Christine Thomson, Thomas Casey, Matt Turner and Nick Turzynski, for their dedication, expertise, good humour and friendship.

I am grateful to my sister-in-law Sue Werry for her thoughtful and insightful comments, and to my husband David who accompanied me on a trip to the Bay of Islands and provided many brilliant images. Thanks also to tutor Adrian Tangaroa Wagner and to my fellow students in our Te Reo Māori classes at Wellington High School.

Lastly, thanks to Creative New Zealand for supporting this work with a Quick Response Grant.